D1559815

COMPLETE BOOK
OF 1-3-1 BASKETBALL

Other Books by Jimmy Earle

Coaching the Flip-Flop
Basketball Offense

Coaching Basketball's Red-Dog Defense

COMPLETE BOOK
OF 1-3-1 BASKETBALL

Jimmy Earle

Parker Publishing Company, Inc.
West Nyack, New York

LIBRARY OF CONGRESS CATALOGING IN PUBLICATION DATA

Earle, Jimmy.
    Complete book of 1-3-1 basketball.

    Includes index.
    1. Basketball.   2. Basketball coaching.
I. Title.
GV885.E18   796.32'3'077   76-13383
ISBN 0-13-157578-3

Printed in the United States of America

Dedication

To my mother and father, Pat and Iva Earle, who raised me
with love, understanding and discipline.
They shall live with me forever.

THE BATTLE OF LIFE

"In the 'battle of life,' it is not the critic who counts; not the man who points out how the strong man stumbled, or where the doer of a deed could have done better. The credit belongs to the man who is actually in the arena; whose face is marred by dust and sweat and blood; who strives valiantly; who errs and comes up short again and again because there is no effort without error and shortcoming; who does actually strive to do the deeds; who knows the great enthusiasm, the great devotion, spends himself in a worthy cause; who at the best knows in the end the triumph of high achievement; and who at the worst, if he fails, at least fails while daring greatly, so that his place shall never be with those cold and timid souls who have tasted neither victory nor defeat."

Theodore Roosevelt

Foreword

It is with a great deal of pleasure that I recommend Jimmy Earle's *Complete Book of 1-3-1 Basketball*.

This book is must reading for the basketball coach in the modern-day game of basketball. It offers the basketball coach a thorough, detailed insight into the most widely used offensive and defensive alignment in the game today.

I consider Jimmy Earle to be one of the most knowledgeable young coaches in the game today. He has been successful wherever he has coached—in high school, junior college and major college. His tremendous won-lost record and numerous coach-of-the-year honors reflect his outstanding basketball expertise.

Gene Bartow
Head Basketball Coach
U.C.L.A.

The How and Why of the 1-3-1 Offensive and Defensive Alignments in Modern-Day Basketball

The 1-3-1 offensive and defensive alignments are probably the most widely utilized and most effective alignments in modern-day basketball. The successful basketball coach of today must either utilize the 1-3-1 offensive and defensive alignments or possess a keen insight and thorough knowledge of both the systems.

The point (one man) offensive and defensive alignment affords the opportunity of providing flexibility in offensive and defensive attacks. This flexibility is of extreme importance to the success of the basketball coach as he constantly has to face the sophisticated offenses and defenses in today's game.

The Complete Book of 1-3-1 Basketball is a concise, detailed and in-depth study of the 1-3-1 offensive and defensive systems that I have utilized successfully during the past 17 years. Both the 1-3-1 offensive and defensive alignments have been successful on three different levels of competition; high school, junior college and major college.

This book contains diagrams and detailed descriptions of 1-3-1 offensive man-to-man maneuvers that are capable of cutting a man-to-man defense to shreds. The modern-day concept of man-to-man offense, referred to as the passing game executed from the 1-3-1 offensive alignment, is discussed for the first time at length in this book. The 1-3-1 offensive maneuvers against zone defenses are clearly diagrammed and explained. These offensive maneuvers have been extremely effective against zone defenses, yielding high-percentage shots and exceptional offensive movement and offensive penetration. An excellent 1-3-1 ball control offense capable of breaking a man wide open during the critical last minutes of a game is clearly discussed. A devastating 1-3-1 controlled breaking game is clearly illustrated and defined. The 1-3-1 full-court offense is capable of scoring over 100 on numerous occasions. The key secrets and techniques of this unique breaking game are unlocked for even the beginning basketball coach.

The various defensive stunts from the 1-3-1 zone are clearly explained through diagrams and step-by-step explanations of each defensive stunt and the theory involved. These defensive stunts are capable of completely neutralizing high-powered offenses and rendering their offensive movement static. The 1-3-1 zone defense that has become the enigma of the modern day basketball coach is fully illustrated and clearly defined. The 1-3-1 trapping defense allows a team to dictate the tempo of a basketball game and in many instances to completely upset an offensive team's rhythm and offensive penetration. The 1-3-1 trapping defense that has become synonymous with the winning basketball teams of today is explained both in theory and execution.

The Complete Book of 1-3-1 Basketball affords the basketball coach an arsenal of 1-3-1 offensive and defensive weapons. The offensive and defensive maneuvers illustrated and explained in this book are capable of turning a defeat into a victory by offering an equalizer against the bigger and stronger teams.

Jimmy Earle

Contents

Chapter 1

The 1-3-1 Offense
Versus Man-to-Man Defenses

The 1-3-1 offensive maneuvers in this chapter are maneuvers we have used with success on three different levels of competition; high school, junior college, and major college. Let me be the first to point out that many of these maneuvers I have picked up over the years from other, outstanding basketball coaches. Since experimentation plays such an important part in modern-day coaching, we have been fortunate in our studies of the 1-3-1 offensive alignment. Before we illustrate and discuss the 1-3-1 offensive maneuvers it is imperative that we discuss the desired player characteristics of each of the 1-3-1 offensive positions.

THE BASIC 1-3-1 OFFENSIVE POSITIONS AND

DESIRED PLAYER CHARACTERISTICS

The Point Position

The point man is the quarterback and the traffic director of the 1-3-1 offensive alignment. He must be an excellent ball handler and passer because he will bear the brunt of the pressure defenses. He will be constantly pressured and harassed all over the court by teams attempting to distract him from his game plan and his point guard responsibilities. The point guard must be able to perform the following offensive maneuvers to relieve pressure: full speed reverses on the dribble; the behind-the-back dribble; the between-the-legs dribble; the stop-and-go cross-over dribble.

The point guard must possess excellent shooting range. It is imperative to the success of the 1-3-1 offensive attack that he be able to shoot the ball from "downtown." By this we mean he must be able to hit a high percentage of his shots from 18 to 20 feet from the basket. He must have a quick release on all his shots. This is especially true for the smaller point guard. In most instances, the smaller guards possess the speed, quickness and ball handling that we are looking for in this position.

The point guard must possess or attain what we call the "Basketball Intellect." By this we mean the ability to read team defenses, the ability to spot and exploit individual defensive weaknesses, the ability to coordinate both the team offense and the team defense and general basketball instinct and savvy.

The Right Wing Position

The right wing position should be played by your best shooter, who in many instances will be your best one-on-one-basketball player. We prefer to play him in the right wing position, because statistics have shown us that there is a tendency to shoot from the right side of the floor more than the left. We also have found that the defense must play our best shooter tight, which affords him a better passing opportunity into the pivot area. By playing on the right wing, he is able to feed the offensive post man inside on his right side. This is very advantageous to the offensive post man as most of them are more proficient when moving to their right.

We will spend a lot of time with our right wing man working on his passing. We stress the two-hand overhead pass for our wing players, but we also work with them on the bounce pass and the swing pass. He must be able to utilize all of these passes effectively.

The right wing man must be extremely adept at utilizing a screen, especially the horizontal screen. On occasions in some 1-3-1 offensive patterns, the wing man will utilize a vertical screen set for him by the low post man, but in most instances the screen he will utilize the most will be the horizontal screen. This type screen will be set for the wing man in most instances by the high post man. The right wing man and the high post man should coordinate their movements through two-on-two offensive breakdown drills in practice. In most instances, the right wing position will be played by the second guard, or the shooting guard.

The right wing position offers an area of the floor from which a high-percentage shot may be taken; therefore, the best shooter is usually placed at the right wing position.

The Left Wing Position

The left wing position is usually filled best by the quick forward or the best shooting forward and the one who possesses the best shooting range. He should be a good rebounder, and a finesse type player if at all possible. He should be a good ball handler and a good one-on-one perimeter basketball player. He should possess good speed; in many instances he will be rotated to the top of the key and be responsible for defensive coverage against the fast break. Since percentagewise our offense will be initiated to the left side of the floor almost as many times as the right, the left wingman should be as equally adept offensively as the right wing man, if possible.

The High Post Position

The high post position should be filled by the best inside one-on-one forward on the team. He should be a capable jump shooter, able to hit a high percentage of short-range jump shots. He should be an excellent driver, able to drive to the basket either to the right or left. He must possess what we term "survival moves" to the basket. By this we mean being able to control his body movements in the air on drives and to shoot the ball while being closely guarded. The high post man should be extremely well coordinated with exceptionally good hands. He should also be an excellent passer, as he will be utilized as a feeder on numerous occasions. His floor position affords him excellent passing opportunities to the other positions in the 1-3-1 offensive alignment.

The Low Post Position

The player at the low post position should be a physical type player possessing much strength in his arms, legs and back. He should be an excellent offensive rebounder as this position affords him good board position. He should be able to execute the offensive maneuvers that are essential for him to be a strong offensive threat. The following are some of the low post offensive maneuvers: a power move; a short left and right hook shot; a short jump shot; a jump hook shot; and a baseline drive with an over-the-head shot. These are just a few of the basic offensive maneuvers the low post man must be able to utilize from this position. We will discuss these offensive maneuvers and fully explain them later on.

The low post man is located in the best offensive floor position in the 1-3-1 offense. In many instances, a coach will place his best offensive player at this position, regardless of his size, and build his offense around him. This will most certainly depend on the individual coach and his coaching philosophy and personnel.

Now that we have discussed the desired player characteristics of each position of the 1-3-1 offensive alignment, we are ready to illustrate and discuss the various offensive maneuvers.

THE GUARD OUTSIDE MANEUVER

The guard outside maneuver is keyed by the point man's cutting route following his pass to the forward. This maneuver affords us many excellent scoring opportunities both inside and outside. It is important to remember that the point man, after his entry pass to the forward, has vacated the point position, thus leaving the key area open. This maneuver can be run at anytime. The defense, in many instances, will dictate when we will run it. If the defensive man who is guarding the point man is pressuring him and forcing him outside, then he can run the guard outside maneuver. We instruct our point man not to fight pressure and to go away from it whenever possible. The following diagrams illustrate the guard outside maneuver.

Whenever we execute any of our 1-3-1 offensive maneuvers, we initiate them with what we term "crackdown" screens. We sprint our wing men 2 and 3 down the floor and position them on the block area (Diagram 1-1).

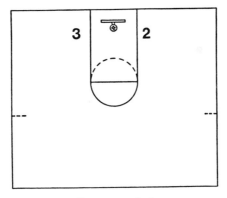

Diagram 1-1

4 and 5, our high and low post men, respectively, then position themselves inside the free-throw line extended with a good screening angle and execute crackdown screens on 2 and 3 positioned on the block areas (Diagram 1-2).

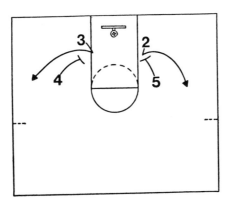

Diagram 1-2

Note: It is important that the crackdown screens executed by 4 and 5 be timed and that 4 and 5 hold their positions until 1, the point man, shows direction with the ball and has penetrated to a good passing angle.

We will, in most instances when utilizing our basic 1-3-1 offense, slide the post man positioned on the ball side of the floor up the lane to the high post position. We are now in our basic 1-3-1 alignment and ready to execute the offense (Diagram 1-3).

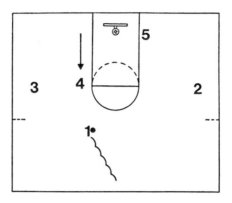

Diagram 1-3

1 makes the entry pass to 3 and executes an outside cut, between 3 and the sidelines. 1 goes all the way to the baseline area and positions himself between 3, the wing man and 4 the high post man (Diagram 1-4).

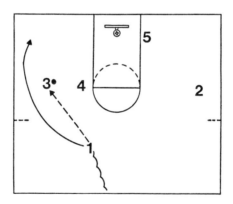

Diagram 1-4

3 upon receiving the pass from 1, squares up to the basket and assumes a triple threat position with the ball. By this we mean that he can shoot, pass, or dribble from this position. 4, the high post man, upon seeing 1 going outside to the baseline, quickly turns inside toward the lane and goes down and sets a screen for 5. 5 sets his defensive man up for 4's screen by moving into the lane area. We tell 5 to "put his head underneath the rim" before breaking off of the screen set for him by 4 (Diagram 1-5).

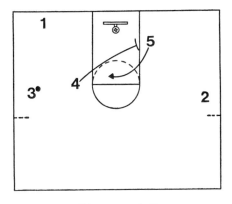

Diagram 1-5

If 3 is able to feed 5, 3 then executes a splitting action with 1 on the baseline. 5, if open for a shot, can shoot a jump shot or he can penetrate with the ball into the lane area. 5 can also pass to either 3 or to 1 coming off of their splitting action (Diagram 1-6).

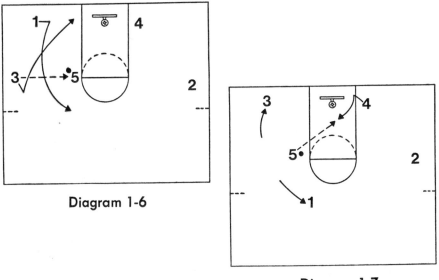

Diagram 1-6

Diagram 1-7

5, after receiving the pass from 3, can also pivot, squaring up to the basket, and pass the ball in to 4 at the low post position (Diagram 1-7).

Note: If no shot is available we are back into our original 1-3-1 offensive alignment.

In the event that 3 is unable to pass to 5 at the high post area, he then looks to the baseline to pass to 1. 1, upon seeing 3 look to him, executes a jab step toward the basket and quickly breaks toward the sidelines to receive a pass from 3. 3 passes to 1 and executes a cut to the basket (Diagram 1-8).

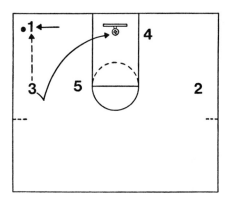

Diagram 1-8

3, after passing to 1, executes a jab step toward the top of the key and quickly cuts to the basket. If 3 is open, 1 passes to him for a lay-up but 3, in most instances, will not be open on his cut to the basket. 1, with the ball, looks 3 all the way through on his cut to the basket. 5, positioned at the high post, holds until he sees 3 is not open to receive a pass from 1. 5 then quickly moves out toward the corner baseline area and sets a screen for 1. 1 utilizes 5's screen and dribbles off of it, and can either shoot a jump shot or execute a screen-and-roll maneuver (Diagram 1-9).

Note: 5's screening for 1 has created a big man-little man situation. In this event, the defense switches on 5's screen. We have created mismatches with 5 rolling to the basket with a guard on him, and 1 coming off the screen with a big man guarding him. This situation gives us a height advantage for 5 rolling to the basket with a guard on him, and a quickness advantage for 1 coming off the screen with a big man guarding him.

If no shot is taken or if a scoring opportunity is not available, it

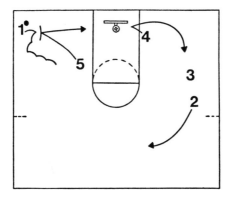

Diagram 1-9

is important that 1 maintain his dribble. 2, the opposite wing man, upon seeing 1 coming off of 5's screen, executes a crackdown screen for 3, who is positioned on the baseline. 3 cuts off 2's screen and 1 passes to him for a jump shot (Diagram 1-10).

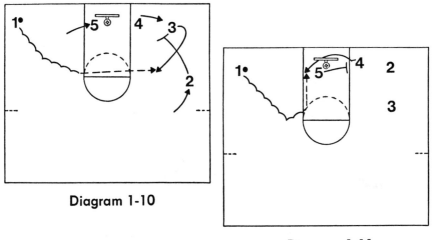

Diagram 1-10

Diagram 1-11

We also have inside screening action developing during this time. 5, after rolling to the basket, moves across the lane and screens for 4. 4 breaks across underneath the basket looking for a pass from 1 (Diagram 1-11).

Note: We have found these last two scoring opportunities to be extremely effective, especially against pressure defenses.

If no scoring opportunities are available, we will regroup by having 2 and 3 quickly sprint to the block areas. 5 and 4 get in their "crackdown" screening position; 1 is already outside at the point position, and we are ready to initiate the offense again (Diagram 1-12).

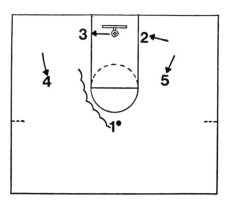

Diagram 1-12

Many teams, after scouting us, overplay the baseline pass from 3 to 1, making this pass impossible. In this case, 3 looks to the vacated point position. 2, the opposite wing man, upon recognizing the defensive overplay of the baseline pass and 3's look to the point area, sprints to the point area to receive a pass from 3. We are not ready to "Reverse" the basektball, and quickly flow into a different segment of our offense (Diagram 1-13).

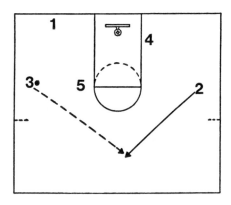

Diagram 1-13

2, upon receiving the pass from 3, quickly turns and looks to pass the ball to 4. 4 sets his defensive man up with a move to the baseline and breaks out to receive the pass from 2 (Diagram 1-14).

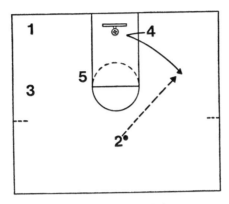

Diagram 1-14

Whenever teams overplay the pass from 2 to 4 and 4's defensive man is pressuring him tightly, we execute a backdoor maneuver. 2 dribbles the ball straight at 4, 4 brings his man two steps higher than usual, plants his sideline foot and quickly executes a backdoor cut to the basket. 2 passes to him for the lay-up. Notice the lane area is open and the defense is vulnerable for the backdoor cut (Diagram 1-15).

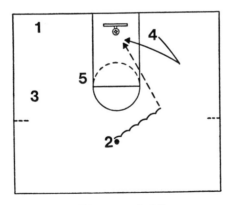

Diagram 1-15

In the event that 2 is able to swing the ball to 4, 3 lines his defensive man up and executes a cut off 5, the high post man, who has moved a step or two down the lane to establish a stationary screen for

3. 3 rubs his defensive man off on 5's stationary screen, and has the freedom to cut off either side of 5's screen. If 3 is open on his cut to the basket, 4 will pass to him (Diagram 1-16).

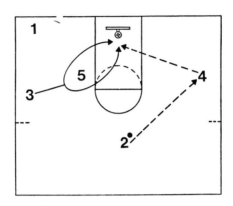

Diagram 1-16

If 3 is not open for a pass from 4, he sets up on the block on the ball side of the floor. 2, after passing to 4, holds his floor position until 3 begins his cut to the basket. 2 and 5 form a double screen for 1, the guard on the baseline. 1, upon seeing 3 execute his cut, moves in toward the lane area setting his defensive man up for the double screen being set for him by 5 and 2. 1 cuts off of the double screen and receives a pass from 4 for a jump shot (Diagram 1-17).

Note: 2 is always on the inside of the double screen and 5 on

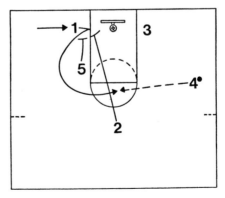

Diagram 1-17

the outside. The timing of 5 and 2 in forming the double screen is of extreme importance. 5 holds his position and waits for 2; they then form the double screen. The double screen should not be staggered, but evenly formed and set at a good angle.

If 1 is unable to receive the pass or receives the pass and is unable to get off a shot, 1 simply moves out to the point position. 2, after helping set the double screen, sets up on the block. 3 is positioned on the opposite block and 4 and 5 are in crackdown screening positions. We are now in position to initiate our offense again (Diagram 1-18).

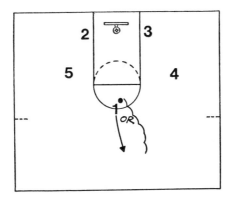

Diagram 1-18

Note: If 1 has the ball and is unable to shoot, he dribbles out to the point position. If 1 is not open for a pass coming off the double screen, he should take his man deeper into the key area and then quickly break out to the point area for the pass from 4.

THE GUARD HANDBACK MANEUVER

This is also an excellent offensive maneuver we have utilized with great success. The key to the success of this maneuver is the timing and execution of the point guard and the wing man. We have found this maneuver to be extremely effective against pressure defenses as it enables us to set a series of screens both on the ball and off the ball.

As we illustrated and discussed earlier, we start all of our offensive maneuvers with crackdown screens. We are now in our basic 1-3-1 offensive alignment and ready to initiate the guard handback maneuver. 1 passes to 3 and executes a dip step following his pass and going outside of 3, 3 pivots and hands the ball back to 1 (Diagram 1-19).

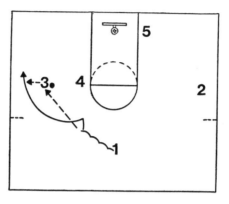

Diagram 1-19

After executing the handoff to 1, 3 has three optional cutting routes. The defense will dictate the route that 3 will take after the handoff to 1. We will discuss each of 3's optional cutting routes and the scoring opportunities afforded by each of them. First, if the defense switches the handoff from 3 to 1, 3 will execute a straight roll to the basket, looking for a return pass from 1 (Diagram 1-20).

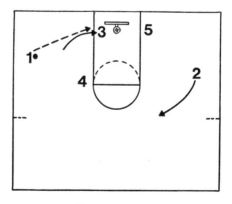

Diagram 1-20

If 1 is unable to pass to 3 rolling to the basket, he then looks into the lane area where 4, after seeing that 3 was not open, has gone down and set a screen for 5. 1 passes to 5 coming off of 4's screen (Diagram 1-21).

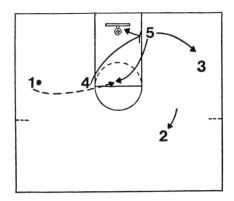

Diagram 1-21

Note: In the event that the defense switches 4's screen, 4 turns and rolls to the basket facing the ball. 1 passes to 4 underneath the basket with his defensive man on his back.

If neither 5 nor 4 is open for 1 to pass the ball to, 5 continues out, screens for 1 and rolls to the basket (Diagram 1-22).

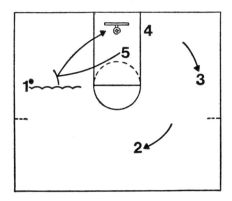

Diagram 1-22

3's second optional cutting route after handing off to 1 is to cut diagonally across and set an inside screen for 4. 4 rolls inside down the side of the lane between the ball and the screen. 1 passes to 4 for the shot (Diagram 1-23).

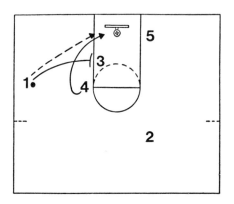

Diagram 1-23

If 4 is not open cutting off of 3's inside pick, 4 continues down and sets up on the block. 3, after screening, goes across the lane and screens for 5 who cuts to the high post. 1 passes to 5 for a jump shot in the high lane area (Diagram 1-24).

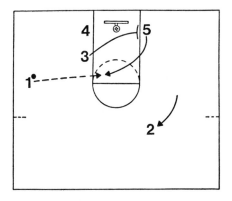

Diagram 1-24

In the event 5 is not open for 1 to pass to, he continues on and screens for 1 as in the first option. 4 clears across the lane, opening up the area underneath the basket for 5 to roll to the basket.(Diag. 1-25)

Note: After screening for 4 and 5, 3 quickly moves out and fills the wing position on the opposite side of the floor.

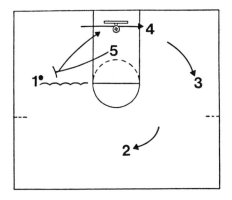

Diagram 1-25

3's third optional cutting route after handing off to 1 is to cut across the top of 4, the high post man, 3 will be open in many instances for a jump shot behind 4's stationary screen, as his defensive man is sagging, expecting him to roll to the basket.

If 3's defensive man is playing him tight after he executes the hand off to 1 and cuts over the top of 4, 3 can quickly cut to the basket. 3 rubs his defensive man off on 4's stationary screen, and can cut to either side of 4 depending upon his defensive man's position. 1 passes to 3 underneath the basket. This is the third optional cutting route for 3 (Diagram 1-26).

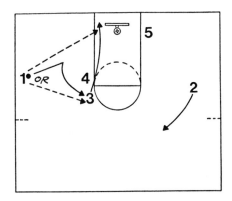

Diagram 1-26

Note: This is a simple offensive maneuver but, with the emphasis on helping on defense, it is surprising how many times 4 will be open for the jump shot.

In the event that 3 or 4 are not open, 3 continues and fills the opposite wing position. 4 moves across the lane and sets a screen for 5 who cuts off of the screen looking for a pass from 1 (Diagram 1-27).

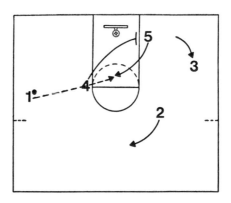

Diagram 1-27

Again as in the previous maneuver, if 5 is not open, he continues out and screens for 1.

3's cut to the basket on many occasions has enabled 4 to be open for a jump shot. 4's defensive man has a tendency to sag deep to help prevent a lay-up by 3. 4 simply pivots facing the ball after 3's cut and receives a pass from 1 for a jump shot.

Note: An important point to stress in the guard handback maneuver is that 1 in some instances may have to utilize his dribble to keep his defensive man occupied and also to prevent a violation.

If no shot is available, we instruct 2 and 3 to go the block areas, 4 and 5 assume their crackdown screening positions and the ball must be passed out to 1 at the point position. We are now ready to begin initiation into our 1-3-1 offensive alignment.

THE GUARD INSIDE MANEUVER

The Guard Inside Maneuver is one of the most difficult to defend against maneuvers in basketball. Coach Guy Strong, Head

Basketball Coach at Oklahoma State University, used this maneuver at Eastern Kentucky University and Kentucky Wesleyan. Coach Strong, in my estimation, has one of the keenest offensive basketball minds in the country.

After we have executed the crackdown screens and we have set up in our basic 1-3-1 offensive alignment, 1 passes to 3, the wing man, and cuts off of 4, the high post man. If 1 is open, 3 passes to him underneath the basket (Diagram 1-28).

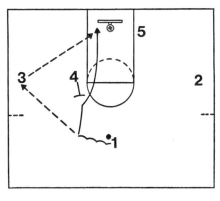

Diagram 1-28

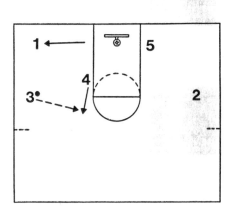

Diagram 1-29

Note: 1 can cut on either side of 4, the high post man, in order to rub his defensive man off 4.

If 1 is not open on his cut to the basket, he quickly moves out to the corner of the baseline on the ball side of the floor. 4, the high post man, times his move and steps out to receive a pass from 3. 4, after receiving the pass, pivots facing the basket (Diagram 1-29).

Note: 4 times his move in stepping out to receive the ball from 3 by holding his position until 1, on his cut to the basket, is two or three steps beyond him. 4's defensive man in most instances will sag back to help guard 1, leaving 4 open to receive an easy pass from 3. 3, upon passing the ball to 4, executes a splitting action with 1 (Diagram 1-30).

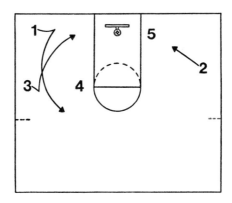

Diagram 1-30

Note: This splitting action by 3 and 1 enables us to keep the defense from sagging in and double-teaming 4.

5, the low post man, upon seeing 4 receive the ball, moves out from his low post position on the block and sets a wide screen for the opposite wing man 2. 2 has moved in toward 5, shortening the distance between them and setting up a good cutting angle. 2 then executes a cut off of 5's screen underneath the basket, 4 passes to 2 for an easy lay-up (Diagram 1-31).

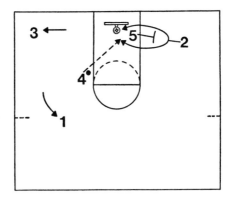

Diagram 1-31

Note: 2 can cut off of either side of 5's stationary screen, depending on the position of his defensive man. We prefer 2 to cut to the baseline side of 5's screen, if possible.

If 2 is not open on his cut to the basket, 4 quickly looks to feed 5. This is one of the most difficult maneuvers to defend against as 5's defensive man must help defend against 2's cut to the basket and then recover to guard 5. 5, after 2's cut, takes one step out from his initial screening position to receive the pass from 4. 5, after receiving the ball, should fake to the middle and if possible drive baseline for a power lay-up (Diagram 1-32).

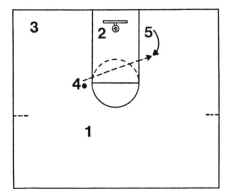

Diagram 1-32

Note: We have found that in most instances 5's defensive man, in recovering to guard 5, is extremely vulnerable to the baseline drive. He has a tendency to recover to the outside in instead of to the inside out.

5, with the ball, is also in an excellent jump-shooting position and in many instances will be open for a quick jump shot upon receiving the ball. 5 should maintain a good floor shooting angle in order to utilize the backboard on his jump shot.

In the event 4 cannot pass to 5 or 5 is unable to get a shot off, the offensive regrouping is simple. 2 sets up on the block on 5's side of the floor, 3 moves in and sets up on the block on 4's side of the floor. 4 and 5 each needs only to move a couple of steps to be in perfect position for their crackdown screens. 1 moves out to the point, looking for the ball.

Many teams will attempt to defend against this maneuver by

instructing the defensive man guarding 4, the high post man, to over-play him and prevent him from receiving the ball from 3. We invite this defensive pressure and have an excellent countermove to neu-tralize it. When 4 steps out to receive the ball and feels the defensive overplay pressure, he comes out one step higher than normal and then quickly executes a backdoor cut down the lane. 5, the low post man, upon seeing 4 cutting backdoor down the lane, flashes up into the high post area. 3 looks first to pass to 4 for a wide open backdoor lay-up (Diagram 1-33).

Note: If 4 is not open for the lay-up, 3 looks to pass to 5 flashing up the lane area. His defensive man may be sagging, hoping to help defend against 4's backdoor cut to the basket.

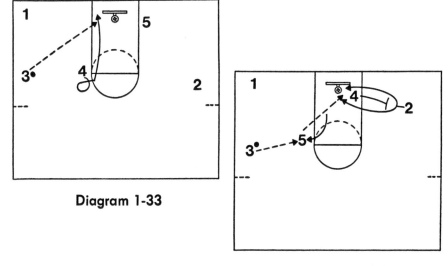

Diagram 1-33

Diagram 1-34

If no scoring opportunity presents itself, 4 after cutting straight down the lane quickly moves across the lane, replacing 5, and sets a stationary screen for 2. 5 who has flashed to the high post area moves out to receive the ball from 3. 2, upon seeing 5 receive the ball, executes his cut to the basket, looking for 5 to pass to him for a lay-up (Diagram 1-34).

Note: The timing between 4 and 5 is of the utmost importance to the success of this countermove against defensive overplay pressure.

THE GUARD SCREEN AWAY MANEUVER

The Guard Screen Away Maneuver is an offensive maneuver that is keyed by the point guard passing to the wing man and cutting away from the ball and screening for the opposite wing man. This maneuver enables us to open up the lane area for cutters coming to the ball.

After establishing our basic 1-3-1 offensive alignment, we initiate the guard screen away maneuver by 1 passing to the wing man 3 and cutting away from the ball. 4, the high post man, upon seeing 1 cutting away from the ball, quickly moves across the lane and sets a double screen with 1 for 2, the opposite wing man. 2 cuts off the top of the double screen looking for a pass from 3. 5, the low post man, maintains his initial floor position and is in excellent rebounding position (Diagram 1-35).

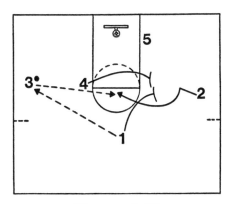

Diagram 1-35

Note: The timing of 1 and 4 in forming the double screen is the key to the effectiveness of the double screen. 4 must be alert and upon seeing 1 passing to the wing man and cutting opposite must move quickly across to the opposite side of the lane to form the double screen with 1.

You will note the lane area and the ball side of the floor have been cleared out by 1 and 4's movement away from the ball.

In the event that a team attempts to defend against this offensive maneuver by switching on 2's cut off of the double screen 1, the top man on the double screen, executes a roll to the basket. 3 passes to 1 underneath the basket for the lay-up (Diagram 1-36).

Note: 1, after receiving the ball from 3, should be alert for 5's defensive man picking him up. If this happens, 1 can quickly pass off to 5 for an easy lay-up.

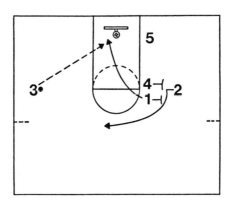

Diagram 1-36

If 1 executes a roll to the basket and is not open, 4 turns and screens down for 5 coming to the ball (Diagram 1-37).

5 will often be open in the lane area for a short jump shot.

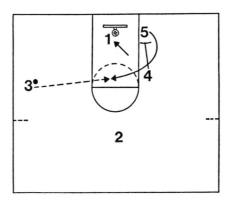

Diagram 1-37

In the event 5 does not receive the ball in the lane area, then he continues high and sets up at a side high post position. 3 passes to 5 at the high post position. 3, after passing to 5, executes a "crackdown" screen for 1, positioned on the block. 1 cuts off the screen looking for a pass from 5. 4 rolls to the opposite block for rebounding position and 2 flares out to the point position (Diagram 1-38).

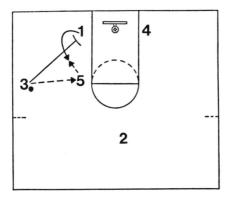

Diagram 1-38

If 1 is not open cutting off of 3's crackdown screen, then 5 has the option of passing inside to 3, who has shaped up on the block after screening for 1, or to 4 who "ducks" in the lane area from the opposite block (Diagram 1-39).

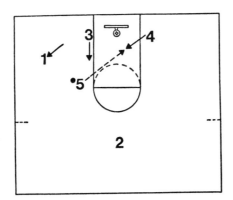

Diagram 1-39

If 2 is being overplayed when cutting off the initial double-screen and cannot receive the pass from the wing man 3, he takes his defensive man one step higher and then quickly back-doors down the lane. 3 passes to 2 for the shot (Diagram 1-40).

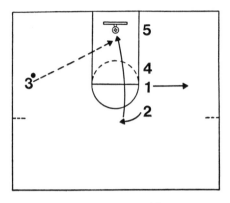

Diagram 1-40

If 2 is not open on his cut down the lane, 1 quickly peels back to the point area and 4 executes his screen down for 5 (Diagram 1-41).

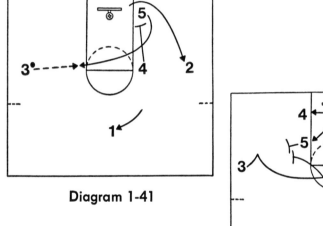

Diagram 1-41

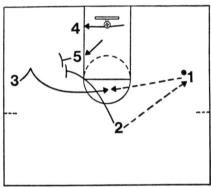

Diagram 1-42

In the event that 3 is able to pass to 2 coming off of the initial double screen and 2 is not open for a shot, he reverses the ball to 1, who has moved out to the wing. 2 then cuts opposite and forms a double screen with 5 for 3, 4 moves away from the ball and 3 cuts off of the double screen looking for a pass from 1 (Diagram 1-42).

THE DRIBBLE INITIATION MANEUVER

This is an offensive maneuver we utilize whenever we are having difficulty initiating our basic 1-3-1 offense against teams that are extremely quick on defense and contest all entry passes into our basic 1-3-1 offense. After the crackdown screen, when we are in our 1-3-1 offensive alignment, we initiate our offense with a dribble instead of a pass. With the popularity and success of the pressure defenses in modern basketball every offense, regardless of the alignment, needs a dribble initiation to get started.

The dribble initiation maneuver is keyed by 1, the point man, recognizing the defensive pressure at the wing position(s) and dribbling straight at the forward 3. 3, upon seeing 1 dribbling at him, quickly executes a backdoor cut clearing out to the other side of the floor where he fills the wing position. 2, the opposite wing man, has moved up and filled 1's vacated point position (Diagram 1-43).

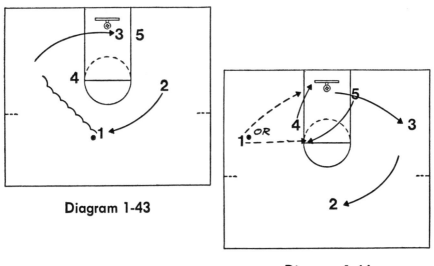

Diagram 1-43

Diagram 1-44

Our inside post rotation is different from the previous maneuvers. 4, the high post man, holds his position until 3 has cleared to the lane area and then rolls down the lane looking for a pass from 1. 5, upon seeing 4 roll to the basket, flashes high also looking for a pass from 1 (Diagram 1-44).

In the event, a shot is not taken or a player is not open for a pass from 1, we now have the players in the following offensive positions (Diagram 1-45).

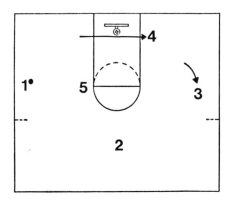

Diagram 1-45

Note: If, after rolling to the block on the ball side of the floor, 4 is not open for a pass from 1, he then clears across the lane to the opposite block.

1 with the ball at the wing position can maintain his dribble. 2 quickly executes the cutting routes of the point guard or 1 can pass out to 2 at the point position and 2 makes the entry pass into the offense. Most of the time we will pass the ball out to 2 and let him initiate the offense.

The Dribble Initiation Maneuver is a maneuver we utilize as a release against pressure defense in order to make the entry pass into our basic offense easier. Although it provides scoring opportunities for the players, its primary purpose is a release against defensive pressure.

THE POST "QUICKIE" SPLIT MANEUVER

This is a special maneuver we have utilized against good pressure defensive teams. We key this visually with the point guard raising a closed fist. 4, the high post man, breaks across the lane to the opposite block; 5, the low post man, breaks high to a high post position in the middle of the free-throw line. It is important to note that this is the only maneuver we utilize with a high post man establishing a position in the middle of the free-throw lane instead of on the side. 1, the point man, passes to 5 and quickly cuts to the basket on the side of the floor where 4, the initial high post man, has vacated. If 1 is open on his quick cut to the basket, 5 will pass to him (Diagram 1-46).

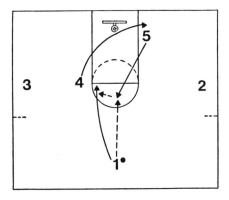

Diagram 1-46

Note: In many instances 1 will not be open initially on his cut to the basket, but if 5 is alert, he can pass to him later down the lane for a lay-up.

After 1's cut to the basket, the wing man on the side of the floor 1's cut was made comes over the top of 5 followed by the opposite wing man. This is a triple splitting action that will enable us to shake either wing man 2 or 3 loose for a jumper. In most instances it is the second cutting wing man who usually is open for the shot.

THE CLEAROUT SPECIAL MANEUVER

This is a special maneuver we will utilize in the course of a game to set up special scoring opportunities for the forward and the point guard. It is also an excellent last-second-shot play and can be utilized at a critical time when a team must have a basket to stay in the ball game.

After we set up in our basic 1-3-1 offensive alignment, the forward on the high post side of the floor, 3, clears out. 5, the low post man, and 2, the opposite wing man, upon seeing 3 clearing out, form a double screen on the baseline. 1, the point man with the ball, has shown direction to the high post man's side of the floor. 1 quickly reverses with the ball and passes to 3 coming around the double screen set by 5 and 2 (Diagram 1-47).

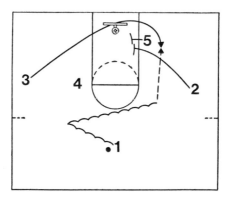

Diagram 1-47

If the defensive man guarding 3 is playing him tight coming around the double screen, then we want him to cut over the top of the double screen rubbing his man off on the top of the double screen (Diagram 1-48).

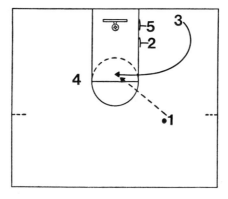

Diagram 1-48

If the defensive man guarding the point man pressures him and will not let him reverse with the ball, 4, the high post man, steps out and sets a screen for 1. They will then execute a screen and roll maneuver to the basket. 1, with the ball, has an excellent scoring opportunity as he has the entire right side of the floor cleared out for him to work one-on-one (Diagram 1-49).

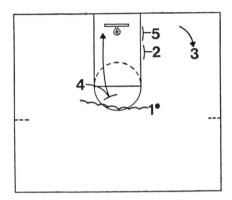

Diagram 1-49

Note: This is an excellent maneuver if the defensive guard out front is in foul trouble. We have had success fouling our opponents' guards out with this maneuver in the latter stages of a crucial game.

The clearout special maneuver can be keyed either verbally or visually. We key it by 1 waving his arm for the wing man to clearout.

Chapter 2

The 1-3-1 Offense
Versus Zone Defenses

The zone defenses in basketball have been the nemesis of basketball coaches for years. In recent years they have become extremely sophisticated with such innovations as the match-up zone, combination defenses, the various stunts utilized with zone coverage, etc. The zone defense has become an important defensive weapon in the modern-day basketball coach's defensive arsenal.

It is of extreme importance to the success of the modern-day basketball coach that he develop a sound multi-zone offense, meaning a zone offense capable of effectively attacking the various zones' defensive coverages. In preparing for the multitude of zone defenses that today's coach is likely to face, it would be virtually impossible to have a special zone attack for each of the complex zone defensive coverages he will face during a season.

With this in mind, we have found that the 1-3-1 offensive alignment is by far the most functional and effective offensive alignment to utilize against both man-to-man and zone defenses. The 1-3-1 offensive alignment offers excellent player floor placement to take advantage of the zone defenses' vulnerable areas, as well as offering flexibility in attacking the various defenses.

There are five important characteristics of a good zone offensive attack. We have incorporated all five of these into our 1-3-1 zone offensive attack. The first is offensive penetration. It is of the utmost importance that the offensive player with the ball (especially the point man and the wing man) penetrate the zone defense with the ball. Offensive penetration with the ball tends to distort the zone defense and force the players in the zone to overcommit defensively, thus leaving them vulnerable.

Second, we want excellent player placement. By this we mean the players' initial floor positions should afford us excellent scoring opportunities from the point area, the wing areas, the high post area and the baseline area. The 1-3-1 offensive alignment offers us scoring opportunities from all of these floor areas.

Third, we want to incorporate excellent ball movement against the zone defenses. Ball movement is important in attacking the zone defenses. Good ball movement forces the zone defenses to shift quickly and in many instances to overshift, thus leaving floor areas in the zone open for offensive scoring opportunities.

Fourth, we want to incorporate excellent player movement against the zone defenses. Player movement is extremely important as an offensive weapon against the more complex zone defenses such as the match-up zones, combination zones, etc. Player movement will create situations with offensive players cutting into the open areas of the zone defenses.

We attempt to probe the zone defenses by constantly cutting offensive players into the areas of the zone probing for the vulnerable areas.

Fifth, screening the zone defense is an effective method of attacking the zone defenses. In years past it was not considered smart basketball to screen a zone defense, and teams utilized screens only against man-to-man defenses. Today, zones have become so sophisticated and complex in their coverage that an effective zone offense must utilize screens against zones. We will screen zones with weak-side baseline screens, usually sending cutters through the zone from the ball side of the floor and swinging the ball around the perimeter looking for the cutter coming off of the baseline screen.

In addition to the characteristics we have emphasized in our 1-3-1 zone offensive attack, the psychological aspect involved in meeting and defeating zone defenses is of extreme importance. It would be well for each coach to weigh the advantages of being mentally prepared to combat any given type of zone defense as it arises during a game situation. The greatest single asset of "preparedness" is the amount of confidence it instills in the individuals and the team as they attack the defense. In many instances, the greatest advantage a zone defense employs is its surprise element or its psychological advantage. The team that employs a multi-zone offensive system to attack all zones has the confidence in its ability to effectively combat zone defenses and immediately eliminates the zone's surprise or psychological advantage and creates its own zone confidence "advantage."

We will now illustrate and discuss the 1-3-1 zone offensive attack that we have utilized with great success on three different levels of coaching—high school, junior college and major college.

THE "SWING" CONTINUITY MANEUVER

The "swing" continuity maneuver is a continuity attack that has excellent offensive movement and has blended in well with, and complements, our other 1-3-1 zone offensive maneuvers.

Diagram 2-1 illustrates our 1-3-1 offensive alignment to attack zone defenses.

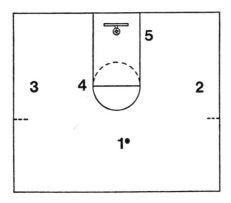

Diagram 2-1

We initiate the swing maneuver from the wing position on the side of the floor where the low post man is positioned. 2, the wing man, receives a pass from 1, the point man, and passes to 5, the low post man, who has moved out toward the corner (Diagram 2-2).

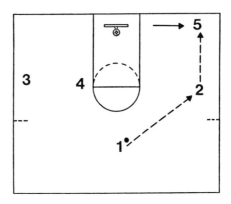

Diagram 2-2

4, the high post man, upon seeing 2 with the basketball, moves across the lane always looking for a pass and a possible score. 2 has the freedom to penetrate the zone, utilizing the dribble and shooting the ball if possible. If 2 is unable to get a good shot, he looks to 5 on the baseline. 2 passes to 5 on the baseline and cuts through the zone looking for a return pass, but in most instances he will not be open. 1, the point man, times his movement and on the flight of the ball from 2, the wing man, to 5, the baseline man, he quickly moves and fills the vacated wing position. In many instances, 2's cut through the zone will cause the zone to sag inward toward the basket to protect, thus leaving the vacated wing area open for a jump shot (Diagram 2-3).

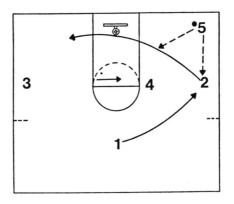

Diagram 2-3

4, the high post man, holds his high post position on the ball side of the floor until 2 has cut to the basket, and the instant 1 has filled the vacated wing position and the zone has expanded back out to protect the wing area, 4 rolls down the lane area looking for an opening and a pass from 5 (Diagram 2-4).

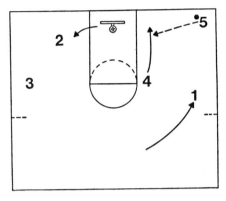

Diagram 2-4

3, the weak-side wing man, flashes to the key or high lane area looking for "daylight" in the defense and a possible scoring opportunity (Diagram 2-5).

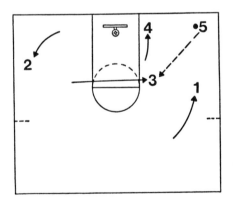

Diagram 2-5

If 3 after flashing into the key area of the zone is not open, he quickly moves out and fills the point position. After flashing into the key area, 3 will hold this position for a two-second count and then move out to the point position (Diagram 2-6).

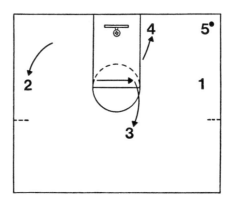

Diagram 2-6

Note: If 5 passes to 3 in the key area, 3 has the option of shooting or passing inside to 4 positioned on the block. In the event no shot is available after 3 receives a pass, 3 passes the ball out to either wing and moves out to position himself at the point position (Diagram 2-7).

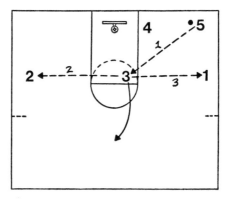

Diagram 2-7

In the event 3 is not open on his flash into the key area and he fills the point position, we swing the ball to the opposite side of the floor. 1 passes out to 3 and 3 passes to 2 positioned on the opposite wing. 4 times his move and moves across underneath the goal to the opposite block looking for a pass. 5 also times his move, moving a few steps toward the basket after passing the ball back out to 2 at the wing position. When the ball is reversed to 3 at the point, 5 cuts up into the lane area looking for a pass. We have had great success with this particular option, especially with 5 being open in the middle of the lane area (Diagram 2-8).

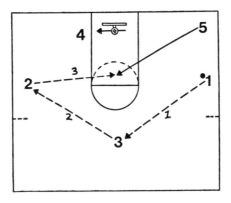

Diagram 2-8

Note: 2 has the better passing angle in passing to 5, although we have been able to pass the ball into him from the point position.

If the ball is reversed quickly and 2 is able to pass to 4 on the baseline and 5 has cut to the middle of the zone, 5 reverses and goes to the opposite block for a possible pass, but more important, for rebounding purposes (Diagram 2-9).

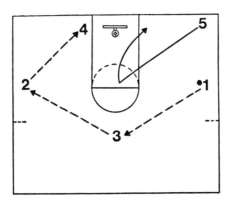

Diagram 2-9

1, the opposite wing man, holds his position until 5 starts his cut to the opposite block and then quickly flashes into the lane area for a possible pass if 4 is unable to shoot (Diagram 2-10).

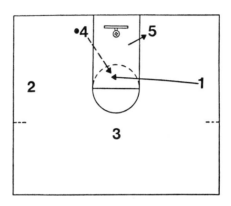

Diagram 2-10

Note: In the event 4 passes to 1, 1 has the option of shooting the ball or passing to 5 positioned on the opposite block underneath the basket.

If a shot is not available after 5 has rolled to block and 1 flashes into the middle of the zone, then the following rotation takes place and we rotate back into our 1-3-1 offensive alignment (Diagram 2-11).

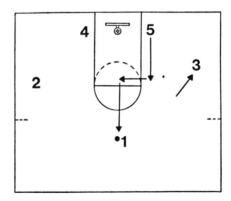

Diagram 2-11

3, in the point position, moves to the opposite wing position. 1, who has flashed to the middle of the zone, quickly slides out and fills the point position. 5, positioned on the opposite block, slides up the lane and fills the high post position. We are now back in our initial 1-3-1 offensive alignment and are ready to run the swing continuity maneuver again.

The swing continuity maneuver is an excellent offensive maneuver to attack zone defenses. It affords us good ball and player movement forcing zone defenses to overshift their defensive coverages. We will now discuss the next offensive maneuver that we utilize against zone defenses.

THE WING CLEAR MANEUVER

The wing clear maneuver combines player movement with weak-side baseline screens and poses zone defenses problems. We have found this maneuver to be extremely effective against match-up zones, combination zones and 1-3-1 zones.

1, the point man, passes to 2, the wing man. 2 passes the ball back to 1 at the point and cuts through the zone. 4, the high post man, upon seeing 2 not passing the ball to the baseline but passing back to 1, the point man, quickly rolls to the opposite block and establishes a screening position (Diagram 2-12).

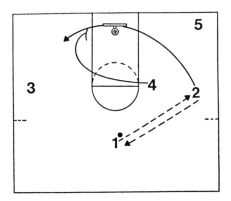

Diagram 2-12

Note: 4's position when the ball is reversed could be established on the same side of the floor as 2. 4 could be in route across the lane or he might still be in his initial position opposite 2. He must get to the block quickly and establish a stationary screen for 2 on the baseline.

1, upon receiving a return pass from 2, utilizes the dribble to improve passing angles, and passes to 3 who passes to 2 coming around 4's baseline screen (Diagram 2-13).

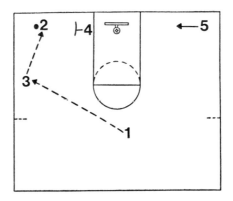

Diagram 2-13

3 also has the passing option of passing inside to 4 who, after establishing the stationary screen, shapes up and establishes a low offensive post position on the block looking for a pass from 3 (Diagram 2-14).

Note: We have found after passing to 2 on the baseline that

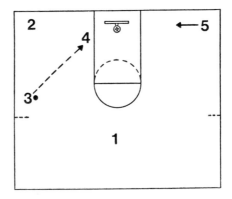

Diagram 2-14

zones tend to overshift in order to defend against 2. 3 can then dump the ball inside to 4 on the block.

Whenever we are playing against lane zones or zones that pressure the wing positions, we have found that 1 by utilizing angle dribble penetration can feed the ball directly into 4. It is important, however, that 4 recognize the pressure at the wings and upon seeing 1 beginning his angle penetration slide up two steps off the block in order to meet 1's pass inside (Diagram 2-15).

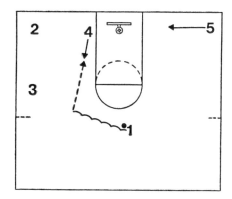

Diagram 2-15

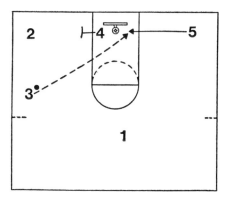

Diagram 2-16

Note: 5, on the baseline opposite the ball, moves toward the basket to assume rebounding responsibilities on the weak side of the floor. We have also, in times past, been able to feed 5 on the opposite block with a diagonal lob pass from 3 or 1, but 3 has the better passing angle (Diagram 2-16).

3, with the ball at the wing position, if unable to find anyone open, passes out to 1, the point man, and cuts through the zone to the opposite baseline. 5, who has moved into the block, establishes a stationary screen for 3 (Diagram 2-17).

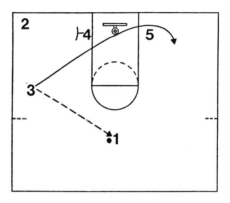

Diagram 2-17

1, after receiving the pass from 3, advances the ball to the opposite side of the floor on the dribble, and passes to 3 cutting off of 5's baseline screen (Diagram 2-18).

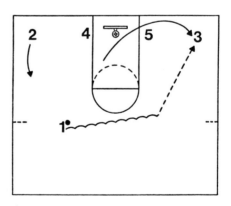

Diagram 2-18

If the zone overshifts to defend against 3, then 1 has the option of passing directly to 5, who slides up the lane to receive the pass (Diagram 2-19).

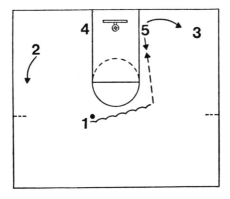

Diagram 2-19

Note: 2 has moved up quickly from the baseline and filled 3's vacated wing position.

If no shot is taken or if 1 is unable to pass the ball to an open man, the offensive rotation is as follows: 3 moves up to the wing position; 5 slides up the lane to a high post position; 2 has moved up from the baseline to the wing position on the opposite side of the floor (Diagram 2-20).

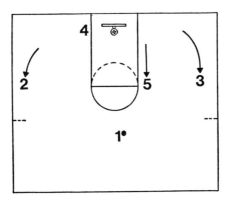

Diagram 2-20

Some zones will not allow us to move the ball to the opposite side of the floor. They will overplay our point man and keep him on the ball side of the floor. We combat this with what we believe to be an excellent countermove, 3 has passed out to 1, the point man, and started his cut through the zone. 2 moves quickly up from the baseline to the vacated wing position. 1, the point man, unable to reverse the ball on the dribble, quickly passes to 2 on the wing. 3 executes a reverse cut and cuts off of 4's screen, 2 passes to 3 on the baseline for the shot (Diagram 2-21).

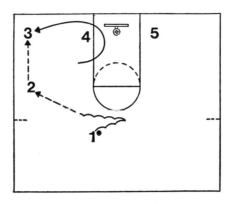

Diagram 2-21

Note: We allow 5 to flash the middle of the zone if he is absolutely sure no shot will be taken.

If a scoring opportunity is not available, 2 will cut through the zone to the opposite wing and 3 will move up from the baseline to the wing position. 4 will slide up the lane to the high post position on the ball side of the floor (Diagram 2-22).

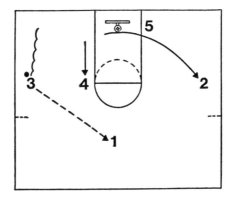

Diagram 2-22

THE "FLOOD" MANEUVER

This is a maneuver we utilize against zone defenses with a dribble initiation by the point man instead of a pass. We have had success with the "flood" maneuver as we are actually "flooding" one side of the zone defense and creating two-on-one offensive scoring opportunities by forcing one defensive player to guard two offensive players.

1 initiates the flood maneuver by dribbling directly at the wing man sliding him down to a position on the baseline (Diagram 2-23).

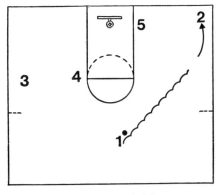

Diagram 2-23

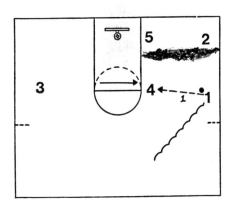

Diagram 2-24

4, the opposite high post man, holds his position until 1 has dribbled to the 2 wing position. He then breaks across the lane looking for a pass from 1 (Diagram 2-24).

1, with the ball, can feed 5 positioned on the block, or 4, who has flashed into the high post area or 2 positioned in the corner on the baseline (this is the last option).

3, the offside wing man, holds his position until he sees 4 is not open and quickly breaks to the top of the key area. He will, in some instances, be open for a jump shot (Diagram 2-25).

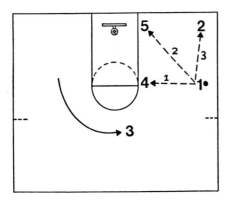

Diagram 2-25

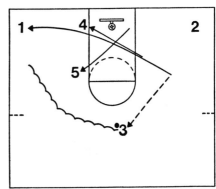

Diagram 2-26

Note: It is important that if a shot is taken, 4 positioned at the high post rebounds the back side of the board.

If 1 cannot find anyone open, he reverses the ball to 3 at the top of the key and runs it to the opposite side of the floor. 1 cuts through the zone to the opposite corner, 3 begins his dribble to the opposite wing position, the post men 4 and 5 execute an X maneuver—4 breaking low to the block area and 5 breaking high to the high post area (Diagram 2-26).

3, with the ball, has the options of feeding 4, 5 or 1, in the corner. 2, positioned on the opposite baseline, has moved in toward the basket and quickly breaks up to the top of the key area completing the rotation (Diagram 2-27).

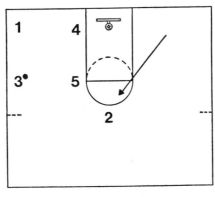

Diagram 2-27

COMBINING THE 1-3-1 WITH THE 1-4 OFFENSIVE
ALIGNMENT TO ATTACK ZONE DEFENSES

When attacking zone defenses we will on occasion rotate from our basic 1-3-1 offensive alignment into a 1-4 alignment. The 1-4 offensive alignment is widely used by coaches across the country and is extremely effective against zone defenses. We have found that by quickly rotating into the 1-4 offensive alignment from our 1-3-1 offensive alignment we have been able to catch zone defenses off balance, thus making our 1-4 offensive maneuvers effective.

The following are the offensive maneuvers we utilize with our 1-4 offensive alignment. First, we will illustrate our simple rotation from the 1-3-1 offensive alignment into the 1-4 offensive alignment (Diagram 2-28).

The movement of one player 5, the low post man, who slides up from the baseline to establish a high post position opposite 4, puts us into a 1-4 offensive alignment. 5 keys, in most instances, on the point guard and upon a visual signal from him moves up the lane into a high post position. 5, himself, on occasion signals the 1-4 alignment to the point guard.

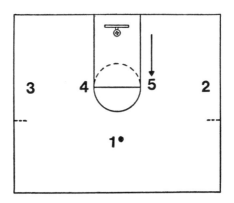

Diagram 2-28

POST EXCHANGES

We will now discuss what we refer to as the "post exchanges" in our 1-4 zone offense. 1, the point guard, can feed either wing, but for illustration purposes he will pass to 2, the right wing man, after passing to 2. 1 goes opposite the ball and interchanges positions with 3, the opposite wing man (Diagram 2-29).

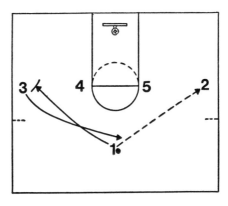

Diagram 2-29

5, upon seeing 2 receive the ball, rolls down the lane and establishes a post position on the block. If 5 is open rolling down the lane, 2 passes inside to him. 4 times his movement and if 5 is not open rolling down the lane, 4 quickly fills his vacated high post position on the ball side of the floor (Diagram 2-30).

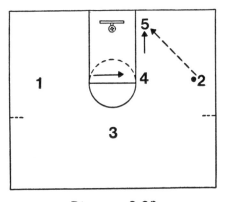

Diagram 2-30

If 4 is open, 2 passes to him at the high post position for a shot or to pass to 5 on the block (Diagram 2-31).

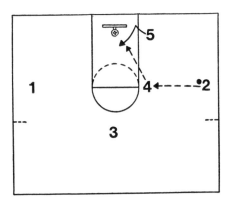

Diagram 2-31

In the event that 4 is not open or a shot is unavailable, we run our post "X" maneuver. 2 quickly swings or passes the ball back out to 3 at the point position. 3 passes to 1 positioned at the opposite wing position. 5, the low post man on the opposite block, seeing 1 receive the pass from 3, quickly breaks to the high post position on the opposite side of the lane. 4 times his movement and breaks off 5's tail underneath the goal to the block area on the ball side of the floor (Diagram 2-32).

1, with the ball has the option of feeding either 5 or 4.

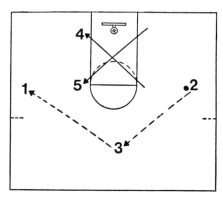

Diagram 2-32

Note: If 1 passes to 4 on the block, 5 will roll back to the opposite side of the board to rebound.

If a shot is not taken, we rotate back into our 1-4 alignment or stay in the 1-3-1 alignment we are in now.

Diagram 2-33 illustrates the rotation back into our 1-4 offensive alignment.

Note: If we want 1 at the point position, we simply interchange 3 and 1.

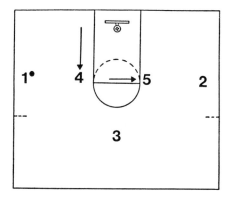

Diagram 2-33

THE "SEAM" MANEUVER

We initiate the "seam" maneuver by the point man passing the ball to a high post man instead of a wing man. We have found this maneuver to be a quick-hitting offensive opportunity that affords us excellent offensive scoring opportunities both on the block areas and from the wing areas.

1, the point man, shows direction away from the high post man he wants to get open for a pass. 1 shows direction to the right and 4 steps out from the opposite high post position to an opening in the zone. 1 quickly passes to 4, and upon receiving the ball, 4 squares up facing the basket and looks to pass to 5, the opposite post man, rolling down the lane area (Diagram 2-34).

Note: 4 will come as high as necessary to get open for a pass from 1.

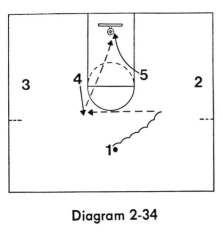

Diagram 2-34

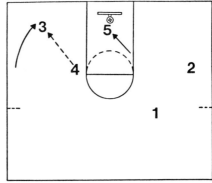

Diagram 2-35

3, the wing man on the ball side of the floor, floats to the baseline area on the ball side of the floor looking for a possible pass from 4 (Diagram 2-35).

In most instances, 3 will not be open for a pass and the corner baseline shot is not a high-percentage shot in our zone attack. The following is our "bread and butter" maneuver. 2 holds his position until 5 has rolled down the lane, 2 then quickly moves into the seam of the zone looking for a pass from 4 and an open jump shot (Diagram 2-36).

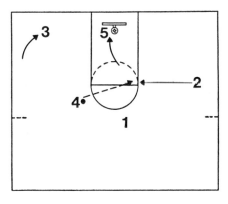

Diagram 2-36

Note: 2 will be open a lot in the seam because coaches instruct the weak-side wing man playing in the zone defense to drop halfway to the basket to protect the back side. This leaves the seam area open.

If 2 is unable to shoot, he has the option of feeding 5 who, after rolling down the lane, has curled across and established a post position on the block (Diagram 2-37).

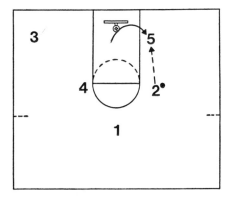

Diagram 2-37

5, upon receiving the pass from 2, has the options of shooting or passing to 4 who breaks straight to the opposite block when 5 gets the ball, or passing to 3 who cuts from the opposite baseline into the vacated middle area of the zone (Diagram 2-38).

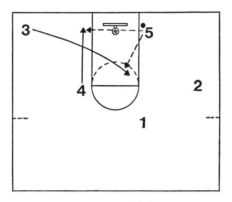

Diagram 2-38

If a shot is not available, we can reset in different manner. We usually have 3 slide out to the point position and 1 move across and fill his wing position. 5 and 4 can both slide high and we will be in our 1-4 alignment, or 5 slides high and we are in our 1-3-1 alignment (Diagram 2-39).

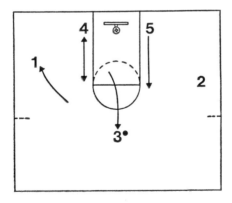

Diagram 2-39

Chapter 3

1-3-1 Offensive Maneuvers in Ball Control Situations

The ability of a team to control the basketball effectively in critical game situations can mean the difference between winning and losing seasons. These situations may arise at almost anytime during the course of a game. Many factors help determine when a team will go into its ball control offense. Such factors as foul ratio, offensive momentum, protection of a lead, attempt to spread the defense out in order to get offensive penetration and playing against superior personnel. Regardless of the factors involved, a basketball coach should develop a sound ball control philosophy. There are various offensive alignments that can effectively be utilized in ball control situations. We believe that the 1-3-1 offensive alignment affords us an excellent ball control alignment and we believe our 1-3-1 ball control game to be extremely sound. The 1-3-1 offensive alignment allows us to go into our ball control game directly from our regular 1-3-1 offensive alignment without having to go into another offensive alignment. In many instances, we can control the basketball for periods of time without our opponents recognizing that we are in our ball control offense. This has been especially true in the early parts of the game.

The timing as to when to utilize the ball control offense has been an age-old nemesis of many basketball coaches. The factors that we mentioned earlier, along with the coach's philosophy concerning the control game, will determine when and how he will utilize his control offense.

The 1-3-1 control offense described in this chapter has been extremely effective for us at Middle Tennessee, and one that we recommend highly as a ball control offense.

THE BASIC BALL CONTROL PATTERN

Our 1-3-1 ball control offense is a continuity type that has excellent movement. Our players are constantly cutting toward the basket and each player is a potential scoring threat.

We initiate our ball control offense in the same manner in which we initiate our regular 1-3-1 offense. We utilize crackdown screens to free our wing men 2 and 3, allowing us to make an entry pass into our ball control offense (Diagram 3-1).

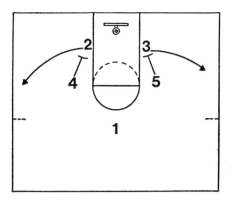

Diagram 3-1

4 and 5, our post men, set the crackdown screen for our wing men 2 and 3, positioned on the blocks. The wing men line up their defensive men for the screen and quickly flare out to their wing positions for the entry pass. The post men 4 and 5, after setting the crackdown screen, assume their identity at the high or the low post (Diagram 3-2).

Note: Whenever we are in our ball control offense, 4 assumes the initial high post position. 4 is more mobile than 5 and in most instances a better passer and ball handler. Since he will be extremely

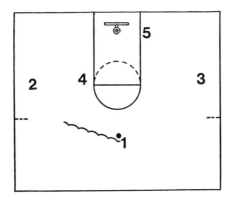

Diagram 3-2

active in the entry into the offense and the early options, it is important that he assume the high post position.

1, the point man with the ball, can initiate the offense to either side of the floor. For illustration purposes, we will initiate the offense to the left side of the floor in the diagrams. We are in our 1-3-1 offensive alignment after the crackdown screens. 1 shows direction with the dribble and penetrates into good passing position (the area slightly to the left of 4, the high post man). He then passes to 2, the wing man who, upon receiving the ball, squares up to the basket and assumes a triple-threat position with the basketball. 4, the high post man, takes a step toward 1 the point man. 1 walks his defensive man toward 4, lining him up, and executes a quick cut to the basket, rubbing his defensive man off of 4's stationary screen (Diagram 3-3).

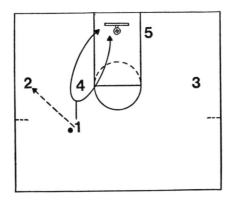

Diagram 3-3

Note: 1, in executing his cut to the basket, may execute a cut to either side of 4's stationary screen. Upon seeing 1 starting his cut to the basket, 5, the low post man, slides two steps off of the block and up the lane (Diagram 3-4).

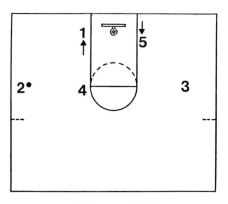

Diagram 3-4

5's movement up the lane helps to take his defensive man away from the basket and also helps to improve passing from 2 and 5.

In the event that 1 is open on his quick cut to the basket, 2 will feed him, in most instances, with a two-hand overhead pass (Diagram 3-5).

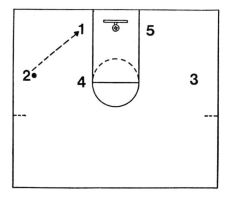

Diagram 3-5

The initial cut by the point man can be executed to either side of the floor. If executed to the opposite side of the floor, 4, the high post man, would move across to the opposite side of the lane to a high post position and 5, the low post man, would move away from the ball.

Note: This cut to the basket by the point man is an extremely important key to the success of our ball control offense as it puts constant pressure on the defense. The direct cut to the basket by the point man forces the defense to honor him without the ball.

After 1's pass and cut to the basket, 4, the high post man, steps out to receive a pass from 2 who has the basketball and has looked 1 all the way through on his cut to the basket (Diagram 3-6).

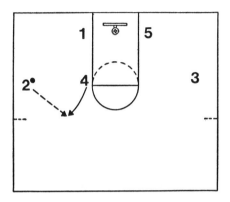

Diagram 3-6

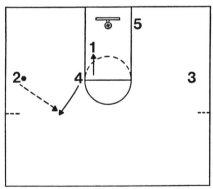

Diagram 3-7

Note: The timing of 4, the high post man, in stepping out to receive the pass from 2 is extremely important. 4 holds his initial position and stationary screen until 1, the point man, on his cut to the basket has penetrated three steps beyond him. 4 then quickly moves out toward the ball side to receive a quick pass from 2 (Diagram 3-7).

4, after receiving the pass from 2, becomes the ball-handling point man. 1, after his cut to the basket, is positioned on the baseline and assumes the responsibilities of the low post position. 5, upon seeing 4 step out and receive the pass from 2, quickly flashes up to, and establishes, a high post position on the ball side of the floor (Diagram 3-8).

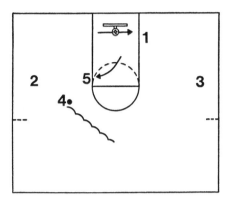

Diagram 3-8

Note: 1, who is now positioned at the low post, should move away from the ball side of the floor. When we are in our ball control offense, it is important that the high and low post men are not positioned on the same side of the lane. This is to maintain good passing angles and to keep the block area underneath the basket open for the point man's cut.

4, who has the basketball, is now the point man and our floor positions are as illustrated in Diagram 3-9.

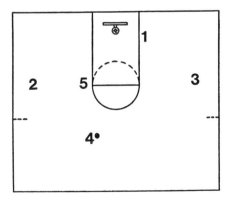

Diagram 3-9

4 can now initiate the offense to either side of the floor. He can feed 2 back and execute a quick cut to the basket, rubbing his defensive man off of 5, the high post man (Diagram 3-10).

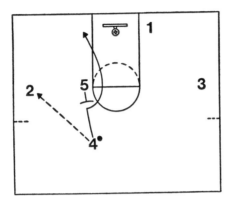

Diagram 3-10

The offensive rotation is the same as the initial rotation: 5, stepping out to the point position; 4 assuming an offensive position on the baseline at the low post; and 1 flashing to the high post position on the ball side of the floor (Diagram 3-11).

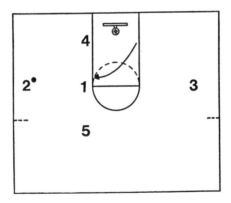

Diagram 3-11

We would prefer 4, after stepping out to receive the pass from 2, to dribble the ball to the opposite side of the floor and pass to 3, the wing man, and execute a quick cut to the baseline. 5, upon seeing 4 dribbling to the opposite side of the floor, moves across the lane and establishes a high post position (Diagram 3-12).

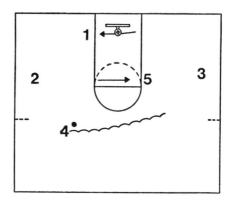

Diagram 3-12

Note: 1, positioned on the baseline at the low post, stays with his rule and goes away from the ball.

4 passes to 3 and quickly cuts to the basket off of 5's stationary screen, and attempts to rub his defensive man off on 5's screen (Diagram 3-13).

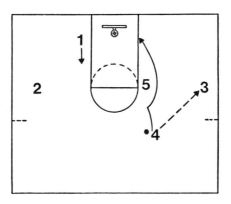

Diagram 3-13

5, the high post man, after 4's cut to the basket steps out to the point position. 1 flashes up to the high post position on ball side. This is the basic offensive rotation in our control game (Diagram 3-14).

This basic offensive rotation has excellent continuity and combined with the proper countermoves places tremendous pressure on the

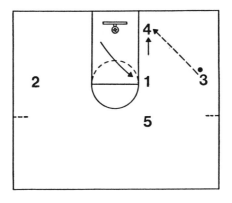

Diagram 3-14

defense. We shall now discuss the offensive counter moves that we utilize to combat pressure defenses.

THE POINT OVERPLAY COUNTER MOVE

Many teams that we play attempt to pressure us out of our ball control offense by overplaying the pass from the wing man to the high post man stepping out to the point (Diagram 3-15).

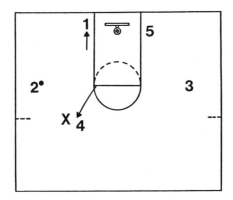

Diagram 3-15

This is an excellent defensive maneuver to upset our offensive rhythm and also if an interception is made, the defensive man has a clear floor for a lay-up. We drill our wing men and high post men to be constantly alert for this defensive overplay.

5, the low post man, must recognize and read the defensive overplay at the point. Upon recognizing the defensive overplay, 5 flashes to the ball and establishes a side post floor position. The offensive countermove that we utilize against defensive overplay at the point is illustrated in Diagram 3-16.

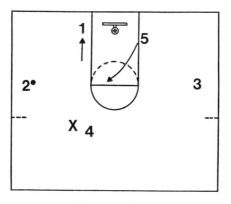

Diagram 3-16

2, the wing man with the ball, unable to pass the ball to 4, the high post man who has stepped out to the point, immediately looks to pass to 5 flashing to the ball (Diagram 3-17).

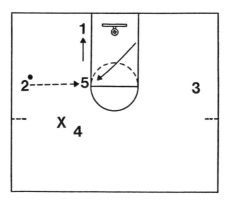

Diagram 3-17

2 passes to 5, 4, upon seeing the ball passed to 5, quickly moves to the opposite wing and screens for 3. 2, after passing to 5, executes a crackdown screen on 1 (Diagram 3-18).

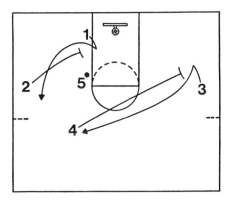

Diagram 3-18

5 has the option of passing to 3 coming off of the screen set by 4 or passing to 1 coming off of the crackdown screen set by 2 (Diagram 3-19).

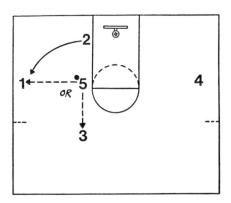

Diagram 3-19

If 5 passes out to 1 at the wing position, we consider that an entry pass into our basic pattern. 2, at the low post position on the baseline, goes to the opposite side of the lane. 3, who has rotated up to the point position, cuts off of 5 at the high post and we are back in the basic pattern of our ball control offense (Diagram 3-20).

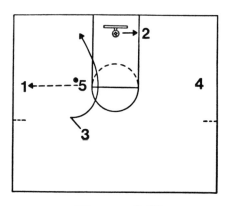

Diagram 3-20

In the event 5 decides to pass out to 3 at the point, 3 will have the option of initiating the offense to either side of the floor (Diagrams 3-21 and 3-22).

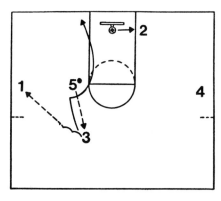

Diagram 3-21

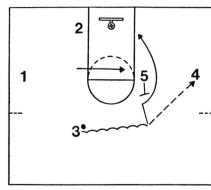

Diagram 3-22

THE INTERCHANGE CUTBACK

An offensive option with which we have scored many quick lay-ups against pressure defenses is a back cut by 3 from the opposite wing off of 4's screen. After the ball has been passed into the post man, who has flashed up to the ball, 4 goes away and sets a screen on 3's defensive man. 3 lines up his defensive man and brings him high as he usually does when filling the point position. He then quickly executes a back cut to the basket, rubbing his man off of 4's screen. 5 passes to 3 backcutting to the basket for a lay-up (Diagram 3-23).

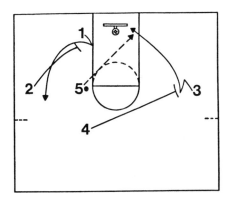

Diagram 3-23

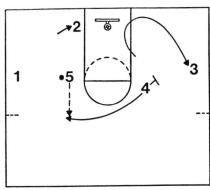

Diagram 3-24

Note: We prefer 5's pass to 3 backcutting to the basket to be a bounce pass.

If 3 is not open for a pass on his backcut to the basket, then 4 quickly breaks to the ball and 5 passes to him and 4 assumes the point position. 3, who has backcut to the basket, peels back and fills the vacated wing position (Diagram 3-24).

Note: In many instances, a team will switch to defend against the backcut. This defensive action can prevent 3 from being open, but allows 4 to be wide open breaking back to the ball to receive a pass from 5.

THE BACKDOOR COUNTER MOVE

Whenever we are in our ball control offense, we will in many instances encounter tremendous defensive overplay pressure at the wing positions. We neutralize this defensive pressure with the backdoor countermove.

Executing the backdoor countermove requires great timing and execution by the point man and the wing man. We can execute the backdoor move to either side of the floor. Diagram 3-25 illustrates 1, the point man, attempting to pass to 2, the wing man, who is being overplayed. 1 executes a good ball fake to 2 to draw his defensive man higher and quickly passes to 4, the high post man. 2, breaks backdoor to the basket and 4 feeds him a bounce pass for a lay-up.

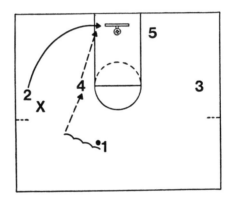

Diagram 3-25

If 2 is not open on his backdoor cut to the basket then the offensive rotation is as follows: 1 fills 2's vacated wing position; 3 moves out and fills the point position; 5 moves out to the opposite wing position; 2, who has cut to the basket, sets up on the baseline at a low post position (Diagram 3-26).

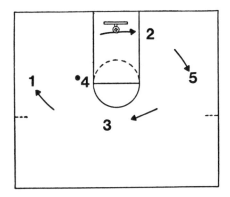

Diagram 3-26

In the event that 1 dribbles to the other side of the floor and cannot make the entry pass to 3, then we run what we call a "quickie" backdoor. 5, the low post man, must read the defensive pressure at the wing and verbally call "quickie" flashing up to the high post for a pass from 1. 3 then back-cuts to the basket and 5 feeds him a bounce pass for a lay-up (Diagram 3-27).

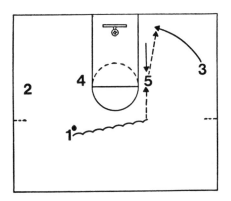

Diagram 3-27

Note: We deviate from the strong-side backdoor we first discussed by allowing 4 to hold his high post position and allowing 5 to flash up the lane for a pass from 1.

The offensive rotation is as follows: 1 fills 3's vacated wing position; 2 moves up and fills the point position; 4 moves out to the offside wing position; 3, who cut backdoor, establishes a position on the baseline at the low post position (Diagram 3-28).

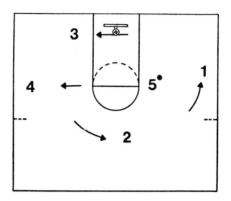

Diagram 3-28

ROTATING FROM THE 1-3-1 OFFENSIVE ALIGNMENT
INTO A FOUR-CORNER ALIGNMENT

On occasions when we are experiencing difficulty handling defensive pressure with our 1-3-1 ball control offense, we will rotate into a four-corner offensive alignment. This offensive alignment tends to spread the defense out and allows us to penetrate with the ball. We

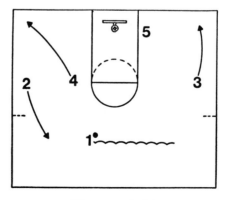

Diagram 3-29

visually signal whenever we want to rotate into our four-corner offensive alignment by the point man holding up an open palm. Diagram 3-29 illustrates the offensive rotation from the 1-3-1 ball control alignment into our four-corner offensive alignment.

We have found that by quickly rotating into our four-corner offensive alignment and opening up the middle we have been able to penetrate the defense and dump the ball off for lay-ups. When we rotate into our four-corner alignment in order to attack zone trapping defenses, guards 1 and 2 should stay spread maintaining good offensive spacing. Forwards 3 and 4 should align themselves about six feet from the baseline and come higher only if needed. 5 should set up on the block and flash to the "Bubble," the key area of the lane when the guards are in trouble and whenever needed.

Chapter 4

The Transitional
1-3-1 Breaking Game

The fast break is one of the most exciting phases of the game of basketball. A well-executed break by a basketball team is a beautiful performance to behold. It provides the team with a devastating scoring weapon that is capable of exploding at any moment and turning a close ball game into a rout.

Here at Middle Tennessee we have installed the transitional 1-3-1 breaking game. We have found this type of breaking game to be very effective and it has been extremely good to us. This style of fast break was originated and utilized very successfully by Sonny Allen, former Head Basketball Coach at Old Dominion and now Head Basketball Coach at Southern Methodist University. Sonny Allen, through his college playing experience at Marshall University under Cam Henderson and his tremendous coaching success at Old Dominion University, is recognized as the foremost authority of the controlled break. Sonny, a close friend of mine, helped me to install our breaking game and I will always be indebted to him for his help.

THE BASIC PHILOSOPHY OF THE BREAKING GAME

In executing the breaking game, its success or failure is highly dependent upon the ball handling of the players involved in the break.

The breaking game in most instances tends to produce more turnovers due to bad passes, floor mistakes and offensive players losing body control. Many players in executing a break will run at speeds where they cannot have full control of their bodies. Also in many instances, in executing a break, a team's poor ball handlers will be involved a lot in the ball handling, thus creating numerous turnovers.

The breaking game we have installed at Middle Tennessee has enabled us to designate the ball handler. By utilizing this concept, we have been able to eliminate many mistakes and turnovers. Our designated ball handler is our point guard, who is our best ball handler. He controls our break and plays at a controlled speed at all times. The other players involved in the break have assigned lane responsibilities and can concentrate almost entirely upon their breaking routes.

One of the most important phases of the game of basketball is called transition. Transition is defined simply as a team's ability to convert from defense to offense, and from offense to defense. Many basketball teams are slow in transition, thus they are more vulnerable to the breaking game. In general, teams have a tendency not to practice and work hard on their transition. The transition from offense to defense is termed by many coaches as the "defensive break." During this period of the defensive break, teams are most vulnerable to offensive penetration, since their defense is spread out over the entire floor. With this thought in mind, we have installed a breaking game that, after the initial thrust of the break, has patterned scoring options that allow us to attack the defense at their most vulnerable points, and also before their defense can be set up. This is the strength of our breaking game, as most of the other breaks that teams are utilizing today have a strong initial thrust, but then are forced to regroup and set up their regular offense. We are able to go directly into offensive options with screening situations, backdoors and splitting situations while the defense is still spread out.

THE ENTRY INTO THE BREAK

We will run our break after both made and missed field goals. Many teams will run only after missed field goals, but we have found that teams tend to relax or loaf after they score and leave themselves vulnerable to the break.

First, let us discuss breaking after a missed field goal. 1, who is our designated ball handler, upon seeing the ball shot always sprints to what we term the "Bubble." The Bubble is located at the free-throw area. 1 should sprint to a spot one step inside the top of the key area (Diagram 4-1).

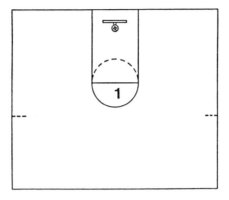

Diagram 4-1

Our rebounders on missed field goals know after gaining possession of the ball to look for 1 inside the Bubble for the outlet pass. In the event that 1 is able to receive a pass inside the Bubble, he is in position in the center of the floor to advance the ball with more freedom (Diagram 4-2).

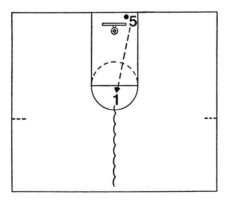

Diagram 4-2

If 1 is overplayed by his defensive man or he is unable to receive a pass in the Bubble, he should sprint to the ball side of the floor and shorten the distance between the rebounder and himself, thus making the outlet pass easier (Diagram 4-3).

Note: In the event that 1 is receiving strong defensive overplay to prevent him from receiving the outlet pass and he cannot maneuver and get open, we instruct him to go to the rebounder and take the ball out of his hands and then start the break. Surprisingly enough, we have still been able to score on teams after 1 had to go all the way to the rebounder to start our break. When we discuss our patterns and offensive options after the initial thrust of our break, you will understand the scoring opportunities provided at the tail of our break.

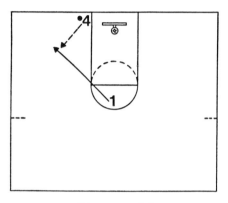

Diagram 4-3

After receiving the ball, we prefer 1 to swing to the right side of the floor in bringing the ball up, if at all possible.

After made field goals we will assign our center or a forward to quickly step out of bounds and throw the ball to 1, our designated ball handler. In most instances, 5, the center, is assigned to throw the ball in after made field goals. 5 is usually closer to the basket than the forwards and can get the ball into play much quicker. The entry into the break is the same as after missed field goals. 1, the designated ball handler, sprints to the Bubble for the inbounds pass from 5. If unable to get the ball, he sprints to 5 for a short pass to start the break (Diagram 4-4).

Note: In executing the inbounds pass to 1, we prefer 5 to throw the ball underhanded (like pitching a softball). This is another point we

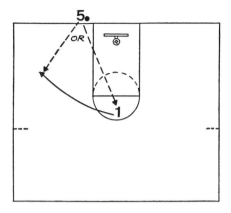

Diagram 4-4

picked up from Sonny Allen. 5, by utilizing the underhanded throw, can control it better and also stop his inbounds pass quicker by bringing his other hand across and putting it on the ball. This happens in many instances when 1 is open and 5 has started his arm motion to pass to him and a defensive player breaks in front of 1 to attempt an interception. If 5 throws a baseball pass, he will be unable to stop the ball, because his opposite arm will be too far away from his throwing arm.

THE LANE ASSIGNMENTS AND THE
INITIAL THRUST OF THE BREAK

Now that we have discussed the designated ball handler and the outlet pass to trigger the break, we will discuss the lane assignment of the individual players and the initial thrust of the break.

We will begin with 2, whom we call the strong guard. He will in many instances release early on a shot and will be open for a long pass and an easy lay-up. 2 should always swing out and fill the right lane. He should run full speed to the block under the goal (Diagram 4-5).

In the event that 2 does not receive an early pass on the break and he is not open on the block, he will then quickly break out to the corner thus opening up the block area underneath the basket (Diagram 4-6).

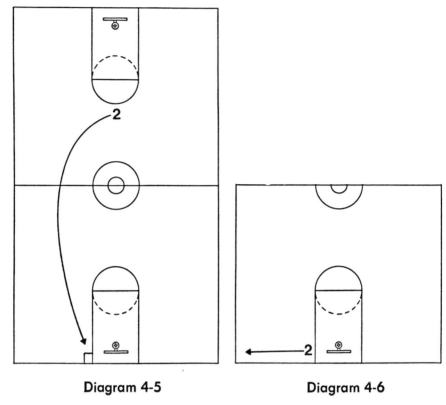

Diagram 4-5   Diagram 4-6

Note: It is important to remember that if 2 releases early he will run a straight route to the block. If not, he will swing wider to open up the middle area of the floor.

3, the quick forward, will fill the left lane and sprint to the opposite block. Since 3 will almost always be involved with defensive rebounding responsibilities he will not release early, but upon seeing us gain possession of the ball will react quickly and fill the left lane, sprinting to the opposite block (Diagram 4-7).

4, the big forward or power forward, upon seeing us gain possession of the ball will swing slightly out to the left side of the floor and fill an imaginary lane between the sideline and the center of the court. He will cut underneath the basket and set up a post position on the block vacated by 2 who has released to the corner (Diagram 4-8).

Note: An important teaching point when working with 4 is to emphasize to him that on his cut to the block he is to swing directly underneath the basket with his head passing underneath the net.

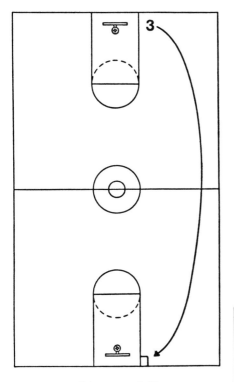

Diagram 4-7

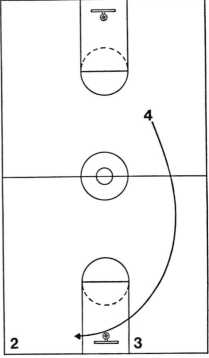

Diagram 4-8

We will discuss the timing of 4's cut to the block underneath the basket after we have discussed and illustrated the individual lane responsibilities of each player.

5, the center, after outletting the ball or seeing a teammate gain possession, should sprint down the floor toward the left side of the mid-court jump circle. He should sprint to the right side of the free-throw line extended and position himself at the second hash mark where the offensive player on free throws establishes position (Diagram 4-9).

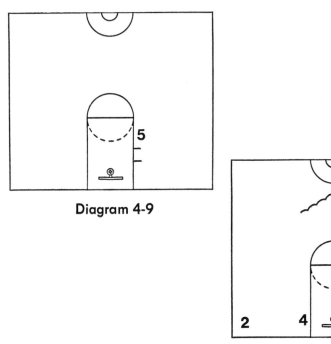

Diagram 4-9

Diagram 4-10

Note: In the conventional break, the center and forwards will be utilized as trailers and will be allowed to shoot jump shots and handle the ball on the initial thrust of the break. We want to utilize our center and take advantage of his strength and inside game, so we have set him up at this position as we will discuss later in this chapter.

Let us now look at the floor position of all the players on the initial thrust of the 1-3-1 transitional break (Diagram 4-10).

1, the designated ball handler, is advancing the ball down the right side of the floor. If 2 is open in the corner, then 1 should come off the ball and feed him a quick pass. 2 has the freedom to shoot if he finds himself wide open or to penetrate by dribbling and distort the defense. In either situation, we have excellent offensive board coverage (Diagram 4-11).

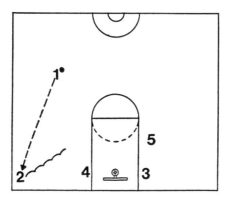

Diagram 4-11

Note: It is important that 2 does not abuse this offensive freedom, utilizes good shot selection and does not dribble, but passes the ball if someone is open inside. The dribble should be used only as a last offensive option by 2.

2, after receiving the pass from 1, should look inside for 4, the power forward, who has established a post position on the block if 4 is open. 2 should then pass the ball to him inside (Diagram 4-12).

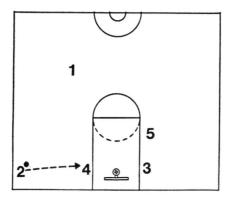

Diagram 4-12

4, upon receiving a pass from 2, has the freedom to utilize his one-on-one offensive moves from the block or post position. 5, the center, upon seeing 4 receive the ball, quickly executes a crackdown screen on 3, who is positioned on the opposite block (Diagram 4-13).

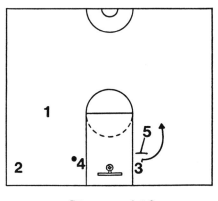

Diagram 4-13

The crackdown screen executed by 5, the center, upon 3 positioned on the opposite block accomplishes two objectives; first, it affords us an excellent offensive scoring opportunity with 3 coming off of 5's screen looking for a pass from 4 and a jump shot. 3's defensive man will in most instances be sagging in the lane area and will be very vulnerable to the crackdown screen (Diagram 4-14).

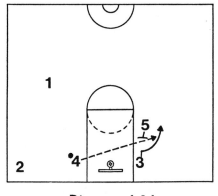

Diagram 4-14

Second, 4 should also be alert to feed the ball inside to 5 who shapes up and establishes a post position on the block after executing the crackdown screen (Diagram 4-15).

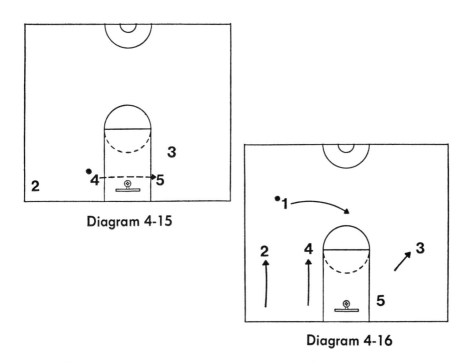

Diagram 4-15

Diagram 4-16

Note: In many instances, 5's defensive man will attempt to double-team or help defend against 4. This leaves 5 open on the opposite block for a quick pass from 4 and if a shot is not taken or is not available from this particular option, we will flow into our 1-3-1 offensive alignment (Diagram 4-16).

THE "PICK-AWAY" MANEUVER

This maneuver has enabled us to get the ball inside to our big people positioned on the block at the tail of our break. Whenever 1 passes the ball to 2, 4 has the option of screening away from the ball. He quickly moves across the lane and sets a screen on 3's defensive

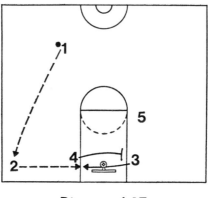

Diagram 4-17

man, and 3 flashes underneath the basket. 2 passes the ball to 3 underneath the basket (Diagram 4-17).

Note: 4 has the freedom to "pick-away" from the ball at anytime. It is automatic for him to "pick-away" whenever his defensive man is fronting him on the block.

Whenever 2 is unable to pass the ball inside to 4 or 3 or to penetrate with the ball, he will pass the ball back out to 1 who will swing the ball to the opposite side of the floor (1 will dribble the ball under control to the opposite side of the floor). 5, the center, positioned on the opposite side of the free-throw lane, times his move and upon seeing 1 dribbling toward his side of the floor executes a crackdown screen on 3 (Diagram 4-18).

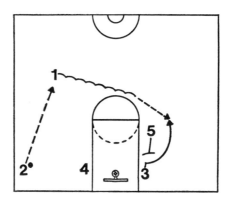

Diagram 4-18

1 is alert to pass the ball to 3 coming off of the screen set by 5. 5, after screening for 3, establishes a post position on the block and attempts to "pin" his defensive man and free himself for a direct pass inside from 1 (Diagram 4-19).

Diagram 4-19

This maneuver is even more effective if executed after the "pick-away" maneuver. By this we mean that if 4 has screened 3's defensive man while 2 has the ball in the corner and then the ball is swung to the opposite side with 5 screening down on 4, it is extremely difficult to defend.

Diagrams 4-20 and 4-21, illustrate the "pick-away" maneuver and the swinging of the ball to the opposite side of the floor.

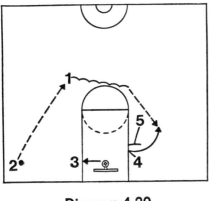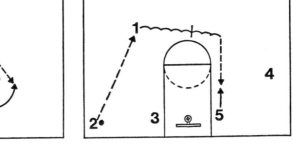

Diagram 4-20   Diagram 4-21

Note: Although 4 is the primary passing target for 1, he should be alert for a direct pass to 5, who has shaped up on the block area after executing the crackdown screen.

1 swings the ball to the opposite side of the floor and passes to 4 coming off of the crackdown screen set by 5. This maneuver places the defensive man guarding 4 under tremendous pressure since he has been forced initially to play post defense on 4 on the block, and second, he must help to defend against the "pick-away" or screening opposite the ball. He is then set up for the crackdown screen set on him by 5. We have found this to be one of the most effective phases of our break.

THE "UP" MANEUVER

We will employ what we term the "up" maneuver whenever teams overplay 2, the strong guard, in the corner and prevent him from receiving a pass from 1. In executing the "up" maneuver, 1, with the ball, signals either verbally or with a waving motion of his off hand to 2 in the corner to move quickly up from the corner to a wing position (Diagram 4-22).

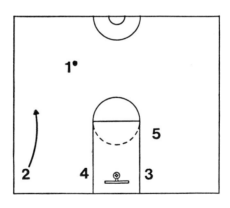

Diagram 4-22

Note: 2 will move to a wing position setting up even with the free-throw line extended and about six feet from the sidelines.

3, who is positioned on the opposite block, upon seeing 2 moving up to the wing position, will break out himself and set up a floor position on the opposite wing. 5 will move down the lane and establish a post position on the block that 3 has vacated (Diagram 4-23).

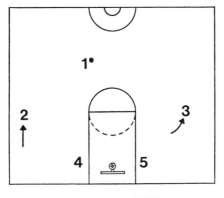

Diagram 4-23

1 will pass the ball to 2 at the wing position. Upon receiving the ball, 2 will face up to the basket and look inside to feed 4 (Diagram 4-24).

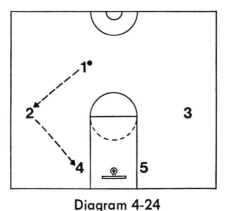

Diagram 4-24

5, the center, positioned on the opposite block, should be alert and "read" the defensive man who is guarding 4 on the block. If 4's defensive man is playing in front of him or is strongly shading the baseline side, then 5 flashes to a high post position on the ball side of the floor (Diagram 4-25).

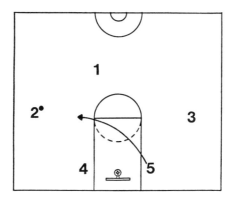

Diagram 4-25

Note: 5, flashing toward the ball and establishing an offensive position at the high post area on the ball side of the floor, has aligned us in a 1-3-1 offensive alignment.

2, with the ball, has several offensive opportunities he can explore. 5, flashing to the high post, has cleared out the back-side area underneath the basket, thus setting up a lob pass to 4 underneath the basket if his defensive man is fronting him (Diagram 4-26).

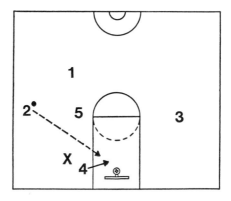

Diagram 4-26

In the event that 4's defensive man is shading him strongly on the baseline side, 2 fakes a pass to 4 to freeze his defensive man on the baseline side. 2 then passes the ball to 5 at the high post. 5 receives the pass and quickly turns and faces up to the basket, and then passes the ball inside to 4, who has his defensive man pinned, rolling across the lane for a lay-up or power move under the basket (Diagram 4-27).

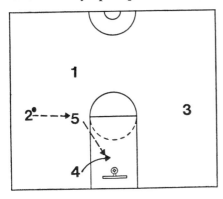

Diagram 4-27

THE "BACKDOOR" MANEUVER

This is a maneuver we will utilize whenever 2 comes out to the wing position and his defensive man continues to overplay him and prevent him from receiving a pass from 1. 4, the power forward, is the key to the successful execution of the backdoor maneuver. 4, positioned on the block, upon seeing 2 being overplayed and prevented from receiving a pass from 1, quickly slides up the lane to the high post position. 1 utilizes a strong ball fake to 2 on the wing to draw his defensive man out to a higher overplay position. 1 then passes to 4 at the high post position. 2 reacts on the flight of the ball from 1 to 4 and executes a backdoor cut to the basket. 4 passes the ball to 2 for the lay-up. (We prefer 4 to use a bounce pass in feeding 2 on his backdoor cut) (Diagram 4-28).

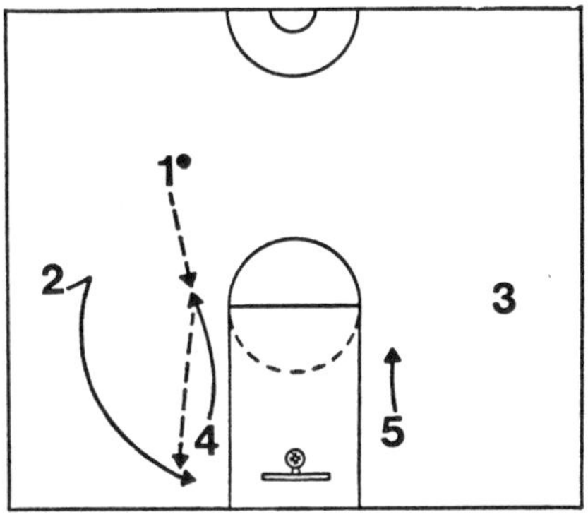

Diagram 4-28

Note: It is important that 5, who is positioned on the opposite block, reacts and on the flight of the ball from 1 to 4, 5 slides up the lane to the high post position on the opposite side of the lane. This opens up the lane area for 2's backdoor cut to the basket (Diagram 4-29).

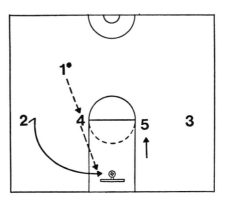

Diagram 4-29

In the event that 4 is unable to feed the ball to 2 on his backdoor cut, he can face up to the basket and work one-on-one. There are several other offensive options that can be run from the "Backdoor" maneuver; these can be developed through the imagination of the coach.

THE "DUCK-IN" MANEUVER

The "Duck-In" maneuver is another inside-oriented offensive weapon we utilize to get the ball to our inside power people. We also initiate this maneuver whenever our 2 man is set at the "up" position on the wing. This maneuver is signaled by 1, either verbally or with a hand signal. 4 slides up the lane as he did in executing the backdoor maneuver to the high post position (Diagram 4-30).

1 passes to 4 at the high post position. 4, upon receiving the ball, quickly turns and faces the basket. 5, upon seeing the ball passed to 4, executes a dip step to the baseline, bringing his inside foot across the defensive man's body. His body is low and his shoulders are parallel to the baseline. 5 gives a target for 4 to pass to with his sideline hand (Diagram 4-31).

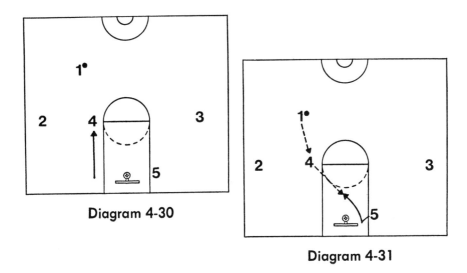

Diagram 4-30

Diagram 4-31

THE POST "QUICKIE" MANEUVER

This is a maneuver that we utilize to counteract any defensive overplay or pressure on 4 whenever he slides up to the high post position. It is keyed by 5, the center, positioned on the opposite block, who reads the defensive overplay on 4 to prevent him from getting the ball. 5 reacts to this situation and quickly slides up the lane to a post position slightly higher than the regular high post position (Diagram 4-32).

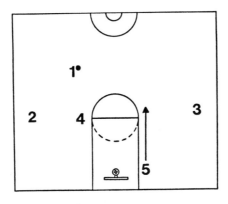

Diagram 4-32

1 fakes a pass to 4 and passes to 5 who has flashed up the opposite side of the lane. 5, upon receiving the pass from 1, quickly feeds a bounce pass to 4 who has cut straight to the basket (Diagram 4-33).

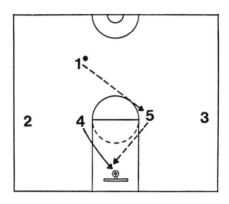

Diagram 4-33

Note: The timing between 4 and 5 is extremely important for the successful execution of the post "quickie" maneuver. It is also important to note that in the event 5 cannot pass to 4, he is free to free-lance with the ball and drive or penetrate to the basket.

Chapter 5

The 1-3-1
"Loco-Motion" Offense

The "Loco-Motion" offense is our free-lance offense, with no primary cutting offensive routes for our players. This type offense is referred to by many coaches as the "passing game." It is an offense widely used by coaches all over the country.

Our Loco-Motion is a free-lance offense with rules that govern our free-lance movement, complementing our offensive movement without hurting its effectiveness. The Loco-Motion encompasses rules that I have picked up from basketball coaches all over the country. I am deeply indebted to Coach Tynes Hildebrand, Head Basketball Coach at Northwestern Louisiana State, for his help and assistance to me in the origination of Middle Tennessee's Loco-Motion offense.

We initiate the offensive movement of the Loco-Motion from a double-crackdown maneuver. We sprint 2, our big guard, to the block, usually on the right side of the floor looking in. 3, our quick forward, sprints to the left block and sets up (Diagram 5-1).

4, our big forward and 5, our post man, align themselves in positions which afford them excellent screening angles. This will be dependent in most instances on the defensive positions of the players guarding 2 and 3 (Diagram 5-2).

Note: 5, our post man should sprint down the floor and align himself on the left side looking in for the crackdown screen. From this

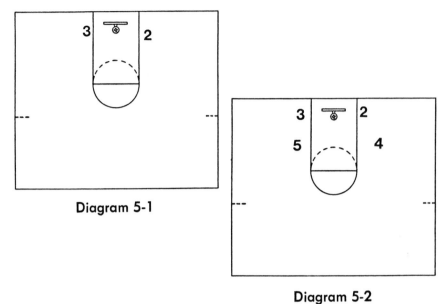

Diagram 5-1

Diagram 5-2

position he will be able to turn inside and use his right hand should he receive the ball.

1, the point man (quarter back) advances the ball straight up the floor without showing too much direction (Diagram 5-3).

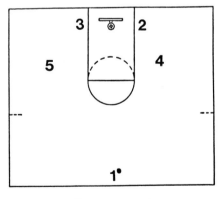

Diagram 5-3

The timing of 5 and 4 initiating the double crackdowns is of the utmost importance. Our rule is as soon as 1 crosses midcourt and shows direction and *is in passing range*, we begin the crackdowns (Diagram 5-4).

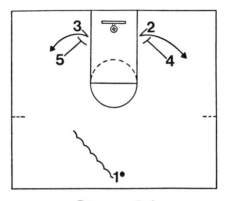

Diagram 5-4

Note: 2 and 3 line their defensive men up with good offensive footwork and fakes and rub them off on 5 and 4 who are executing crackdown screens on them. They may come off the screens either to the outside or to the inside.

After 5 and 4 crackdown, 2 and 3 come off the screens looking for a pass. If they do not receive the ball, they should come out wide to open up the lane area (Diagram 5-5).

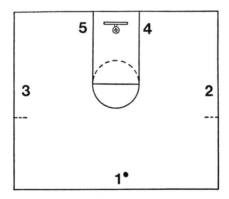

Diagram 5-5

From this alignment we designate 1, 2, and 3 as perimeter players. 4 and 5 are designated post men or interior players. It is important to the successful execution of our offense for the perimeter players 1, 2, and 3 to maintain 15-foot spacing (+ 8 feet from high post).

Note: The coach must constantly use the term "spread" to remind the perimeter players to maintain their 15-foot spacing, and allow more floor area inside for 4 and 5 to operate.

We revolve into our 1-3-1 offensive alignment from the crackdowns with three different maneuvers with our interior players 4 and 5.

The following are the interior maneuvers we utilize to revolve into our 1-3-1 offensive alignment. They are utilized first for scoring opportunities for 4 and 5 and secondly to rotate us into our offensive alignment.

SHAPE-UP MANEUVER

After the double crackdowns, the interior player on ball side shapes up for position on the block (for illustration purposes we will initiate to 5's side of the floor (Diagram 5-6).

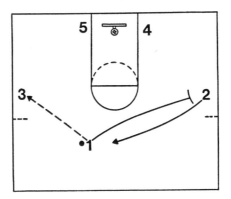

Diagram 5-6

When 5 shapes up on the block looking for a pass from 3, who has just received a pass from 1, 4's movement is keyed by 5's defensive man. If 5's defensive man is fronting 5, then 4 flashes to the high post position on ball side (Diagram 5-7).

Note: 4 flashing high takes the back-side defensive help away and allows us to lob the ball to 5.

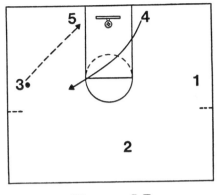

Diagram 5-7

Also, 5 shapes up for a count of three seconds and then vacates (Diagram 5-8).

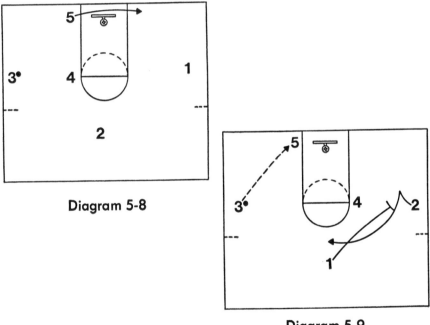

Diagram 5-8

Diagram 5-9

In the event 5's defensive man is playing him from behind, 4 slides high to opposite side post (Diagram 5-9).

4 is now in position to float to the center of the lane for a jump shot in the event his defensive man attempts to double-team 5 who has the ball on the block (Diagram 5-10).

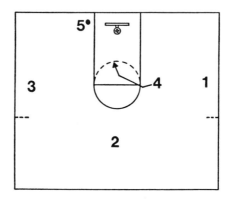

Diagram 5-10

SCREEN AWAY MANEUVER

Our interior players utilize the screen away maneuver in most instances when their defensive men are playing baseline side. (Diagram 5-11).

5, the post man on the ball side turns and sets a screen across the lane on 4's defensive man. 4 comes across the lane looking for a pass from 3 and a lay-up.

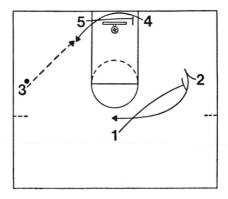

Diagram 5-11

5, after screening 4's defensive man, turns and flashes back to the high post on ball side (Diagram 5-12).

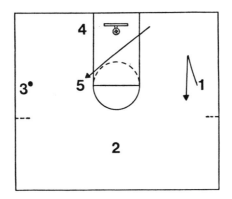

Diagram 5-12

UP MANEUVER

This is an excellent maneuver to utilize against a strong defensive pressure overplay, especially at the wings. 5, after utilizing the crackdown screen, slides up the lane on the ball side of the floor. 5 calls out verbally "up," so as to alert 4 to hold his position on the opposite block (Diagram 5-13).

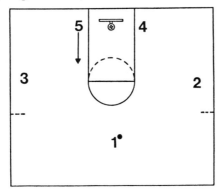

Diagram 5-13

Note: 5 must read strong defensive overplay on 3 during the crackdown screen and call "up." He can now be utilized as an outlet by 1. In many instances, we utilize a backdoor maneuver from this maneuver (Diagram 5-14).

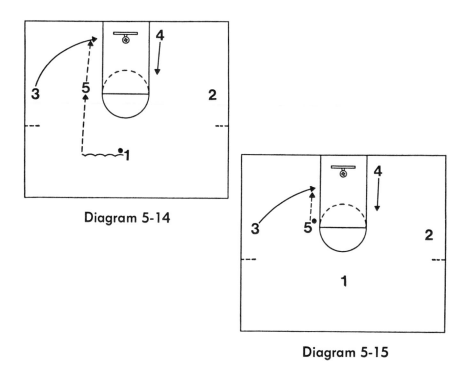

Diagram 5-14

Diagram 5-15

Note: 4, upon seeing 5 receive a pass and a backdoor cut by the forward, moves up to a mid-post position (Diagram 5-15).

After the initial crackdowns, we look to pass the ball inside to our interior players or post men 4 and 5. If they are not open and nothing has developed, we are in our 1-3-1 offensive alignment and go to our "Loco-Motion" offense.

"LOCO-MOTION" OFFENSE RULES
FOR OFFENSIVE MOVEMENT

This offense is an offense that is predictated upon ball movement and man movement. Ball movement, however, is the key to the success of the offense. Dribbling is used only to: (a) improve passing angle; (b) drive ball to basket; and (c) change position of ball.

When receiving a pass from a teammate, a player should look inside. He should maintain possession for a two-second count. This will enable him to observe and take advantage of offensive opportunities that are developing both inside the lane area and around the perimeter of the floor. Passing is the key, but we require our players to look for the open man before passing the ball. After passing, we never follow our pass. (This is a rule you may want to change.)

General Rules

1. You must move every time a pass is made.
2. Look to pass first, shoot second, and drive third. (Think pass.)
3. After offense is initiated, do not utilize more than 3 dribbles.
4. Always make the easy pass.
5. Offensive movement begins when 1, the point guard, shows direction and penetrates into passing range.
6. Anytime you are overplayed, cut to the goal or screen for a teammate. (We prefer cutting to the goal.) ·
7. "V" cut (wing) to receive the ball.
8. All cuts must be executed sharp and definite.
9. Establish inside game first.
10. Move with a purpose, look where you are going—don't make two consecutive cuts in same direction.
11. Maintain good floor balance. Don't congest areas.
12. When ball is passed to post area or shot, designated rebounders think rebound . . . designated defenders think defense (*stop the break*).

RULES FOR PERIMETER MEN

(#1, #2, and #3)

Pass and Screen Opposite

This rule applies to the point man after passing the ball to a wing. He vacates the point screening for the opposite wing who replaces him at the point position (Diagram 5-16).

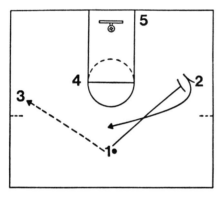

Diagram 5-16

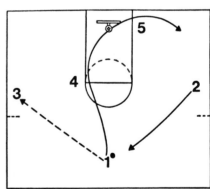

Diagram 5-17

Pass and Cut to the Basket

The point man feeds the wing and cuts to the basket either on a straight cut or using the post man as a rub. He will, in some instances, be open for a return pass, but mostly his cut is to vacate the point position, to be filled by offside wing man 2 (Diagram 5-17).

Pass and Slide

This maneuver is almost the same as the pass and screen away, except there is no screening situation involved. The point man feeds the wing and slides (moves) to an open area of the floor opposite the ball (Diagram 5-18).

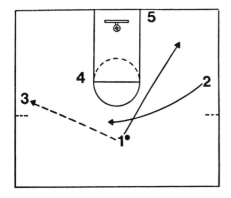

Diagram 5-18

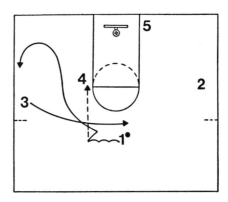

Diagram 5-19

Pass to High and Split

This rule is imperative to the success of the offense. Whenever the ball is passed inside, splitting action by the perimeter players will force the defense to adjust and not permit them to "sag" on the post man (Diagram 5-19).

Pass to Low and Split

The same rule is applicable in this situation, except the ball is passed into the low post (Diagram 5-20).

Note: The player who feeds the post is always the screener. He should stay wide and make a wide, not a tight, split. (This will jam up the floor area.)

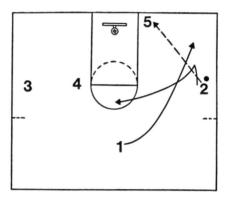

Diagram 5-20

Pass and Clear Out (Wing)

This maneuver is excellent against defensive pressure. The wing man with the ball has the option of clearing out after a pass to the point or the high post (Diagram 5-21).

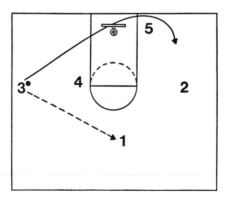

Diagram 5-21

Note: This creates an excellent 2-on-2 situation with 1 and 4. 4 could screen for 1 and roll to basket (Diagram 5-22).

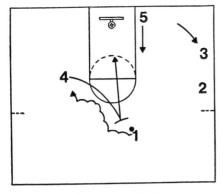

Diagram 5-22

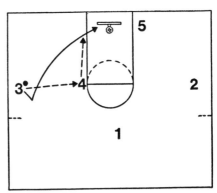

Diagram 5-23

Pass and Clear Out (Wing)

In this situation, 3 passes to the high post and clears out the baseline (backdoor). This maneuver is an excellent scoring opportunity for the wing player (Diagram 5-23).

Note: 3, wing man, feeds high post man 4 and cuts backdoor, receiving a release pass from 4.

Pass and Screen Down (Crackdown)

This offensive maneuver is utilized whenever 4, the high post man, has rotated to the low post. The Pass and Screen Down is an excellent offensive maneuver against a sagging man-to-man defense. It affords 4 an excellent scoring opportunity, freeing him for a jump shot coming off of the screen-down (crackdown) set by the wing man, 3 (Diagram 5-24).

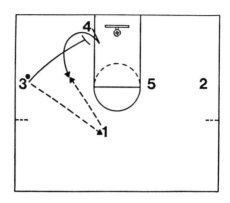

Diagram 5-24

The wing man, 3 in this instance, has the option of clearing out or utilizing the screen-down maneuver on the 4 man.

Many teams who use the motion offense or passing game have a general rule that enables wing players to screen-down on any player who is set up below him during any stage of the offensive movement. We prefer our rule of screening only for the 4 man who is usually the best jump shooter, also leaving 5, our post man, in the lane area for rebounding purposes.

RULES FOR INSIDE MEN

(4 and 5)

High Post Screen for Low Post

This maneuver is initiated by the high post man 4 whenever 1, the point man, passes to a wing man and goes opposite (Diagram 5-25).

Wing man 3, upon receiving a pass from 1, faces up to the basket and looks inside for 5, the low post man coming off the screen

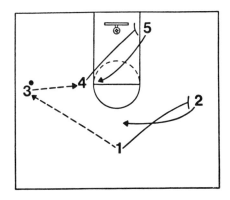

Diagram 5-25

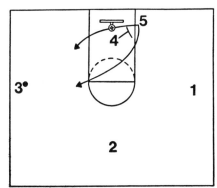

Diagram 5-26

set by 4, the high post man. 5 has the option of coming off of the screen set by 4, either over the top or on the baseline side (Diagram 5-26).

High Post Slide Low

This is an excellent free-lance post-up move for the high post man. It is also initiated by the point man passing to the wing man and going opposite. High post man 4 slides directly down the side of the lane to the block, where he shapes up and establishes a post position looking for a pass from the wing man (Diagram 5-27).

4, the high post man, upon establishing a post position on the block, attempts to pin his defensive man on his back enabling him to be open for a pass from the wing man 3.

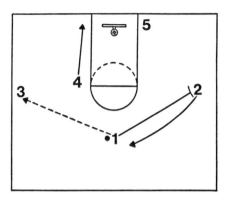

Diagram 5-27

5, the low post man, upon seeing 4 sliding low to the block flashes to the vacated high post position. In many instances, 5 will be open for a pass and a possible scoring opportunity. In the event he is not open, this maneuver has removed the back-side defensive man and enables 4 to have more freedom on the block (Diagram 5-28).

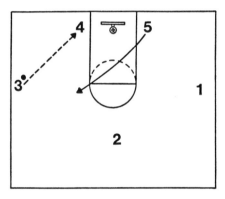

Diagram 5-28

Note: 4, in establishing a post position on the block, should shape up with a wide stance and use his arms to signal a passing target for a pass from 3. In the event that the defensive man plays in front of 4, 3 can lob the ball to 4 as the area underneath the basket has been vacated by 5 (Diagrams 5-29).

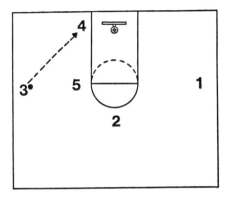

Diagram 5-29

On many occasions 3 can pass to 5 flashing high for a quick jump shot or 5 can face up to the basket and pass to 4 shaping up in the low post area (Diagram 5-30).

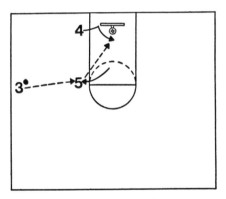

Diagram 5-30

High Post Goes Low If Ball Goes to Low Post

A rule we have for our high post man, which has been very successful for us, is whenever the ball is passed to the low post man, the high post man quickly rolls low to the block opposite the ball (Diagram 5-31).

Diagram 5-31 also illustrates the ball being passed into the low

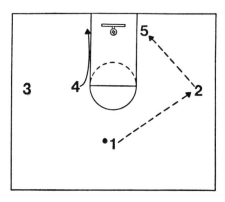

Diagram 5-31

post man 5 by wing man 2. High post man 4 rolls to the block, looking for a pass from 5 and a possible scoring opportunity. It also enables high post man 4 to establish good rebounding position on the opposite side of the board.

Diagram 5-32 illustrates the same rule and maneuver, but with the high and low post men in positions on the same side of the lane.

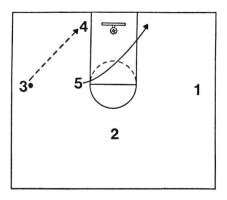

Diagram 5-32

3 passes the ball to 4 who has become the low post man. 5, who has flashed to the high post on the ball side of the floor, upon seeing the ball passed low, turns and quickly peels off to the block on the opposite side of the lane.

Note: The low post man should be alert for this quick movement by the high post man. He should utilize the bounce pass in feeding the high post man.

Back Screen for High Post Man

The back screen is a maneuver that is initiated by the low post man. Whenever the ball is passed to the wing and the high post man is on the ball side of the floor, the low post man can execute a back screen on the high post man.

In order to co-ordinate movement between the two post men, the low post man uses a verbal key to alert the high post man he is going to set a back screen for him. We use the verbal key of "RED" to signal for the back screen.

This maneuver is excellent for freeing the high post man for a lay-up. We have found it to be extremely effective against aggressive pressure man-to-man defenses (Diagram 5-33).

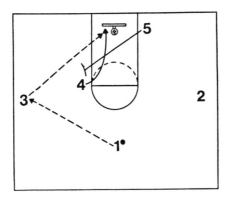

Diagram 5-33

1 passes to 3, the wing man. High post man 4 is positioned on the ball side of the floor. 5, the low post man, hollers the verbal key "RED" and quickly moves toward the high post man. He sets a back screen on 4's defensive man. 4 rolls off the back side of the screen and wing man 3 lobs the ball to him under the basket.

Note: 3, the wing man, in passing to 4, the high post man after a back screen has been utilized, should utilize a lob pass as he will be passing over tall interior defensive players.

The back screen is also an excellent maneuver, not only as a scoring maneuver, but to open or free the high post man against pressure defenses (Diagram 5-34).

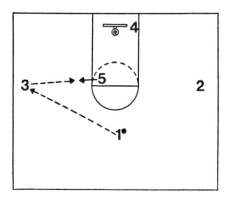

Diagram 5-34

5 has executed a back screen for 4, the high post man, 5 then steps toward the ball looking for a pass from wing man 3. In most instances, 5 will be wide open for a pass after executing a back screen, as his defensive man will be sagging in the lane area to protect the basket area.

HIGH POST MAN WITH THE BALL

(Rules Governing His Movement)

One of the prime objectives of the "Loco-Motion" offense is to get the ball to our high post man. He is the hub of our offense and with the ball he can generate many scoring opportunities since he has the better passing angles, as well as the high-percentage scoring area.

The ball may be passed to the high post man either from the point man or the wing man. An important rule to remember is that whenever the ball is passed to the high post man, the player who passed the ball executes a splitting-the-post maneuver. The splitting action should maintain a spacing of from 8 to 12 feet from the high post man.

Diagram 5-35, illustrates the point man 1 feeding high post man 4 and executing a splitting action with 3.

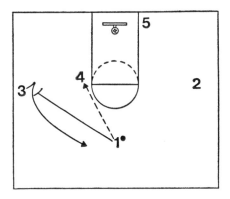

Diagram 5-35

Note: 1 passes to the high post man and quickly breaks to screen 3. 3 dips to the basket and cuts around 1's screen. Again, let me emphasize the importance of maintaining the 8-to-12-feet spacing and not congesting the high post area.

Diagram 5-36, illustrates wing man 3 feeding 4, the high post man, and executing a splitting maneuver with 1, the point man.

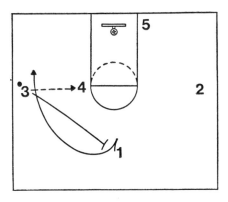

Diagram 5-36

3, the wing man, passes to the high post man and breaks to screen for 1, the point man. 3 breaks after his pass to screen for 1, the point man, who has dipped toward the basket and cuts off of 3's screen.

Note: As mentioned earlier in the chapter, perimeter players should maintain 15-feet spacing from each other. This will enable them to execute splitting situations much more effectively and help them to maintain the 8-to-15-feet spacing on all splits.

If a defense player is guarding either the point man or the wing man, the high post man should be alert to pass the ball off to the offensive player coming off of the split.

Note: It is important that the offensive player alert the high post man verbally that he is open.

We will now discuss and illustrate the various scoring options the high post man has with possession of the ball at the high post position.

Upon receiving the ball, the high post man should first face up to the basket, pivoting on his inside foot (the foot next to the lane area). This enables him to work from the "triple threat" position. By this we mean he can shoot, pass or dribble from this position.

High Post Man Feeding Low Post Man

This maneuver has been extremely good to us. It enables us to really put pressure on the defense and has helped to create early foul problems for our opponents.

Diagram 5-37 illustrates 4, the high post man, with the ball facing up and feeding 5, the low post man, who has "Ducked In." By this we mean he has his defensive man pinned on his back.

Note: 5, the low post man, should time his movement and upon seeing the high post man begin his pivot with the ball, take his

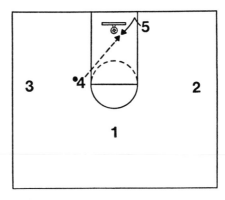

Diagram 5-37

defensive man to the baseline and cross his inside foot (the foot closest to the lane area) across in front of the defensive man, thus enabling him to ''pin'' him on his back. This stance should be low with the shoulders parallel to the baseline. The sideline shoulder should be lower than the inside shoulder. The feet should be spread and arms widely extended for position and also to signal a passing target.

The passing angle, in most instances, is to the outside as the defensive player will be fighting to protect the lane area (Diagram 5-38).

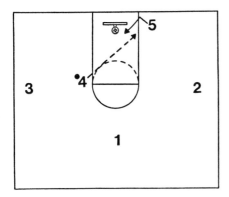

Diagram 5-38

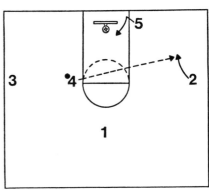

Diagram 5-39

From this position we want 5 to operate one-on-one and be extremely aggressive with the ball. We want him to power the ball into the basket.

In the event that 5, the low post man, is not open, the high post man with the ball looks to the weak-side wing man 2 to pass to. He will, in many instances, be open as his defensive man will be sagging to protect the lane area (Diagram 5-39).

High post man 4, after feeding 2 on the weak-side wing, has many offensive options he may execute.

Note: 2, if open for a jump shot, has the freedom to shoot from his wing area. This is especially true if it is 2 who is our scoring guard, playing on the right wing.

High post man 4, after passing to the weak-side wing man, may screen on the ball or screen away from the ball and execute what we term a "post-loop."

Diagram 5-40, illustrates the high post man, after feeding the weak-side wing man, setting a screen on the ball.

5, the low post man, after seeing 4 pass the ball to 2, clears across the lane away from the ball. 4 moves across and sets a screen on 2. 4 and 2 execute a screen and roll maneuver.

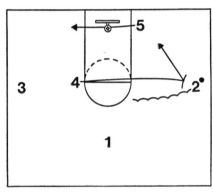

Diagram 5-40

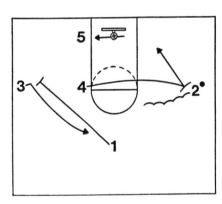

Diagram 5-41

Point man 1 and wing man 3 may interchange during this maneuver. 3 may be in the point position and 1 in the wing position. This does not matter; the interchange can still be executed. Diagram 5-41 illustrates the total movement from this option.

If no scoring opportunity develops from this option, then we can regroup.

The following diagrams illustrate the high post man screening away from the ball.

Diagram 5-42 illustrates the high post man screening for 3, the opposite wing man.

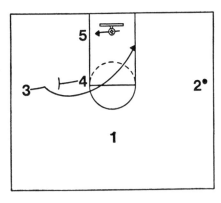

Diagram 5-42

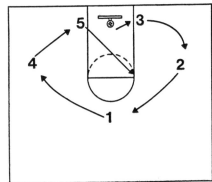

Diagram 5-43

4, the high post man, steps out and sets a wide screen for 3, the wingman, who cuts off of him to the basket to receive a pass from 2 and a possible score.

Note: In regrouping, we use a rule that is very flexible. FILL THE POSITION ON THE FLOOR WHERE YOU ARE NEEDED.

Diagram 5-43 illustrates a method of regrouping after this particular option.

4, after screening, rolls low and sets up on the block. 5 moves up to the high post position on the opposite side of the lane. 1 and 3 will set up at either the point position or wing position, depending on their original positions. 2, the wing man, with the ball, remains at the wing position or fills the point position.

Diagram 5-44 shows the high post man screening away from the ball for the point man.

4, steps out and sets a screen for 1, the point man, who cuts to the basket looking for a pass from 2 and a possible score.

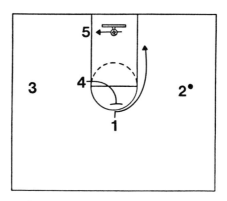

Diagram 5-44

Diagram 5-45 illustrates the high post man executing the post "loop" maneuver. The post loop has been an extremely successful scoring option for us and has enabled us to get the ball to our inside players with relative ease.

4 rolls to the open block area on the ball side of the floor, looking for a return pass from 2 and a score. This maneuver by the high post man will be effective if the high post man executes a good fake away from the ball and then cuts to the block.

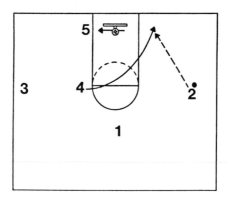

Diagram 5-45

5, the low post man, upon seeing 4 cutting to the block, flashes to the high post area on the ball side, thus opening up the area on the back side of the basket (Diagram 5-46).

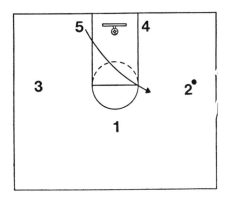

Diagram 5-46

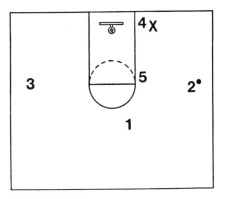

Diagram 5-47

In the event that 4, the high post man, is not open on his cut to the block, 2, the wing man with the ball who is looking to feed 4 on the block, fakes a pass to him. This fake will freeze 4's defensive man, usually bringing him up on the baseline side of him (Diagram 5-47).

Note: The defensive player (x) guarding 4 on the block reacts to a pass fake from wing man 2 and moves up on the baseline side of 4.

2, after his pass fake to 4 on the block, feeds 5 at the high post. 5 quickly turns and feeds 4 who has pinned his defensive man on his back and rolled across the lane (Diagram 5-48).

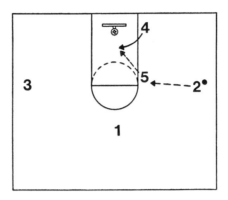

Diagram 5-48

"SPECIAL" OPTION

The "Special" option is an option we installed and utilized against ball clubs who depended upon back-side sagging defensive help to stop the inside game of our Loco-Motion offense.

This option is initiated by the 1, the point man, passing to the wing and cutting to the corner on the ball side. This movement violates our basic offensive rule of passing and cutting away from the ball, but we have found it necessary and it has added to the effectiveness of the offense against ball clubs who are highly dependent on back-side defensive help (Diagram 5-49).

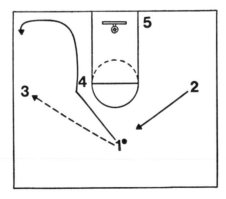

Diagram 5-49

1, the point man, passes to 3, the wing man and cuts to the corner on the ball side of the floor. 2, the weak-side wing man, fills the point position. 5, the low post man, upon seeing 1 cut to the corner on the ball side of the floor, moves across the lane flashing toward the ball, looking for a pass (Diagram 5-50).

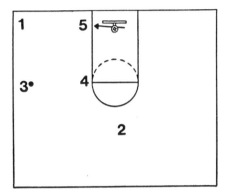

Diagram 5-50

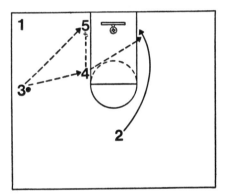

Diagram 5-51

Note: This maneuver has removed all defensive back-side help and allows us to exploit the lane area with more freedom. Post men 4 and 5 can move with more freedom.

Diagram 5-51 illustrates the various passing angles and cuts we can run from this offensive maneuver.

Note: 2 can, in many instances, run a backdoor cut to the basket, executing a backdoor cut from the point position.

Chapter 6

The Modern
1-3-1 Zone Defense

The 1-3-1 zone defense has become increasingly popular among the basketball coaches of today. It can be devastating against modern offenses if played as aggressively as the coach decides to teach it. This particular zone can be played as a drop-back, basket-type defense or as an aggressive defense with pressure both on and off the ball. We prefer to teach and utilize it as an aggressive, pressure-type defense.

The following are the defensive floor positions and player characteristics desired at each defensive position. Diagram 6-1 illustrates the 1-3-1 zone defense and the numbers we utilize to denote each position.

THE POINT MAN OR "MONSTER" MAN

1, the defensive point man, we refer to as the "monster man." We give him this name because we want him to scare the offense. The defensive point man is our first line of defense and we want him to be extremely aggressive and possess good court awareness. We would prefer 1 to be 6 feet 2 inches or taller, but in many instances he will be your smallest player. Some coaches will put their smallest player on

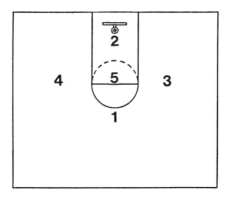

Diagram 6-1

the baseline. We have played him at both places and feel it depends upon the individual player. If he is a quick, aggressive-type player, we want him on the point as our monster man.

1 should limit his defensive coverage from lane to lane early in practice, until he becomes familiar with the position. Diagram 6-2 illustrates the lane-to-lane coverage.

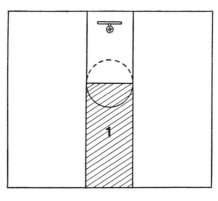

Diagram 6-2

Note: We refer to this lane-to-lane coverage area as 1's cage. We want 1 (the monster man) to remain in his cage most of the time.

After 1 becomes familiar with his position then he will be able to attack offenses and increase his defensive range and responsibilities.

The key to the success of the point man or the "monster man" is mixing up his techniques and positions on the floor in which he attacks the offense. Sometimes he needs to attack the ball at mid-court. Another time halfway between the circle and the mid-court area. Another time, two steps from the top of the key area. He should attack the ball vigorously and then again fake to the ball and cover the opposite guard.

Diagram 6-3 illustrates the various floor areas of attack for the point man.

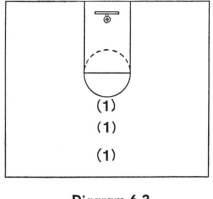

Diagram 6-3

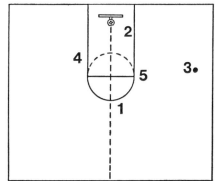

Diagram 6-4

The point man can initially set up and attack the offense from various defensive positions on the floor. He can set up at the mid-court area, 3 steps back from the half-court. His initial defensive setup can be between the mid-court circle and the top of the key. His initial defensive setup position can also be a tight position two steps from the top of the key area. In the event he is playing against a one-guard offensive front he should put tremendous pressure on the offensive point man to keep him from penetrating and changing sides of the floor with the ball. One of 1's basic responsibilities is to isolate the ball and keep it on one side of the floor. The ball should never be allowed to move across the court to the opposite side of the floor on a direct pass (a line drive-type pass). Diagram 6-4 shows the court divided into two parts to illustrate keeping the ball on one side of the floor.

Note: In the event the offense does reverse the ball to the opposite side of the floor, they should be forced to use a bounce pass or a lob pass. These passes are the slowest passes in basketball and allow the defensive players more time to move in the 1-3-1 zone to change their defensive responsibilities.

1, the "monster man," can influence the ball to the side of the floor he desires. In most instances, the scouting report will dictate in which direction 1 should influence the ball.

THE LEFT WING MAN OR "POWER" MAN

4, the left wing man on the 1-3-1 zone defense, or the "Power" man as we refer to him, should be your best rebounding forward. In some instances, 4 will be your slowest player, but by placing him on the left side of the floor, he will not be as vulnerable to offensive attacks, as most teams initiate their offenses to the right side of the floor. 4's body position should be with knees slightly flexed, hands up and spread high above his head, with his arms moving in a circular motion as rapidly as possible.

4's floor coverage responsibility is one step above the free-throw line extended on the ball side of the floor (Diagram 6-5).

Note: We will cover higher depending on our scouting report, but in most instances we will designate one step above the free-throw line as our maximum line of defensive attack for our wing man.

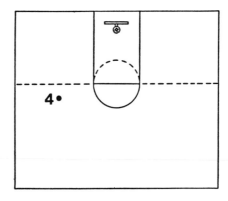

Diagram 6-5

One of the most important defensive responsibilities of 4, the left wing man, is maintaining a good body angle in relationship to the ball. 4's body angle should always be such as to prevent a direct pass from the top of the key to the baseline (Diagram 6-6).

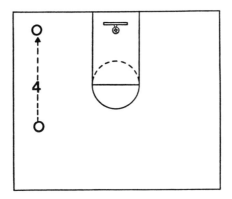

Diagram 6-6

4 should attack the ball handler high and stop him from penetrating. Again, his body angle is extremely important. He should take away the passing lane to the baseline. His body angle will be largely dependent upon where an offensive player is positioned on the baseline (Diagram 6-7).

Note: 4 should maintain a body angle on the ball to prevent a direct pass to the offensive player positioned on the baseline.

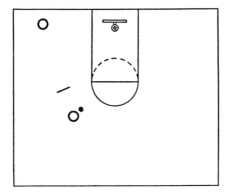

Diagram 6-7

He should approach the ball in the "attack" position (knees slightly flexed, arms extended over his head, waving in a circular motion). His inside foot should be aligned slightly on the inside of the outside shoulder of the ball handler. His feet should be spread and his outside foot extended.

Whenever 4, the left wing man, is playing away from the ball as in Diagram 6-8, his first responsibility is to protect the block (basket area). He aligns himself in what we term the "quiver" position (halfway between the basket area and the free throw-line extended).

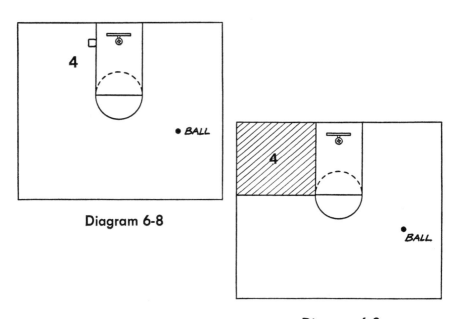

Diagram 6-8

Diagram 6-9

4, whenever playing opposite the ball, should alter his stance. By this we mean his stance will not be the same as when he is pressuring the ball.

Diagram 6-9 illustrates 4's defensive floor coverage.

Note: 4's first defensive responsibility is to protect the block (basket area). However, he has the freedom to attempt to intercept a cross-court pass. He must utilize good judgment in attempting interceptions; if the cross-court pass is a lob pass or bounce pass 4 should feel free to attempt an interception.

Another important factor in determining 4's freedom in attempting to intercept cross-court passes is the degree of penetration by the offensive team. In the event a team is penetrating our 1-3-1 zone, 4 or the wing men should be hesitant about going for an interception. On the other hand, if a team is not penetrating and is attacking our 1-3-1 zone from the perimeter, 4 should be alert for interception possibilities. When playing opposite the ball, 4 will have more floor coverage responsibility. Therefore, his stance should be adjusted to allow him better vertical movement. His body position should be lowered, knees flexed, arms lowered with inside arm extended toward lane area and below shoulder level. The outside arm should be raised and extended outward to discourage a pass to opposite corner. This stance enables 4 more freedom of movement and allows him much more defensive range.

THE CENTER OR "HUB" MAN

5, the center, is the "Hub" of the 1-3-1 zone defense. His defensive responsibilities require quickness and mobility. If 5 is slow or hesitant in executing his defensive responsibilities, it usually results in a lay-up for our opponents.

5's major defensive responsibility is to stop offensive penetration. He must react to offensive penetration from any angle on the floor.

Diagram 6-10 illustrates 5's defensive positioning in our 1-3-1 zone defense.

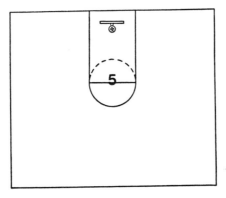

Diagram 6-10

When the ball is out front, 5 usually positions himself at the free-throw line. His initial defensive position is dependent upon the defensive positioning of 1, the monster man. The higher 1 comes out to attack the offense, the higher 5 must come up to stop penetration.

Diagram 6-11, illustrates 5's defensive floor area responsibility.

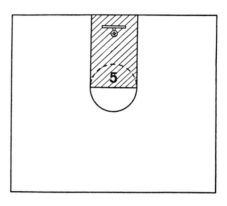

Diagram 6-11

Note: 5 is responsible for the lane area and one step around the outside of the lane area. This coverage will be explained later in the chapter.

The most difficult defensive maneuver and responsibility of 5 is that of stopping offensive penetration out front and then sprinting to protect the block or the basket area. 5 should front any offensive player in his area; he should play between the offensive player and the ball. He must not allow anyone to get the ball in the lane or pivot area of the floor.

Diagram 6-12 shows 5 stopping penetration from the point area and sprinting to protect the block or basket area.

The offensive player has attempted to penetrate from the point of the zone area. 5 has come up quickly to help stop the penetration. The offensive player passes the ball to a teammate on the baseline. *Important:* 5, on the flight of the ball, sprints to protect the block or basket area. He fronts the offensive player who has set up on the block.

Note: This defensive maneuver is very difficult and should be practiced daily. Many teams will attack the 1-3-1 zone in this manner.

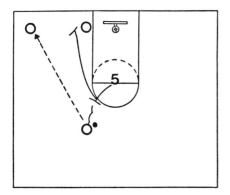

Diagram 6-12

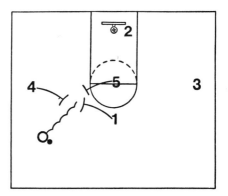

Diagram 6-13

If 5 does not react, it will result in a lay-up for the offensive player stationed on the block area.

Diagram 6-13 illustrates an offensive player attempting to penetrate the 1-3-1 zone from the front. Note 5 coming up to help stop the penetration.

5, upon seeing the offensive player putting the ball on the floor, reacts to the ball and quickly attacks the penetration with his arms up and feet spread. He should apply good pressure on the ball and extend his chest toward the ball. 5, upon helping stop the offensive penetration, must recover as quickly as possible and protect the lane area.

It is important that 5 stop offensive penetration from all areas of the floor. He must react to stop penetration at the point area, the wing area and the baseline area.

THE RIGHT WING MAN OR THE "QUIVER" MAN

3, the right wing man, is our smallest or quickest forward. He is our best defensive forward and since he is positioned on the right side of the floor, he will have to defend against the brunt of the frontal offensive attack.

3, the right wing man's defensive responsibilities are the same as those of 4, the left wing man. His defensive floor coverage area is one step above the free-throw line extended (Diagram 6-14).

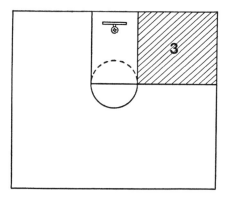

Diagram 6-14

3's defensive approach in guarding the ball should be at an angle in order to prevent the direct pass to the baseline. His stance should be the same as that of 4, the left wing man, whom we discussed earlier in the chapter. His defensive responsibilities are also the same as 4's. The main exception is that we allow 3 more freedom while playing off the ball. His quickness will enable him to anticipate and intercept passes more often. 3 must also be much sounder fundamentally in the execution of his defensive responsibilities, as he will be guarding the ball more often on his side of the floor.

THE BASELINE MAN OR "ROVER"

2, the baseline man in the 1-3-1 zone should possess, if possible, exceptional speed, good lateral movement and should be a good "anticipator." In our 1-3-1 zone defense we play a guard on the baseline at the 2 position. We feel that a guard, in most instances, can fulfill the responsibilities of the baseline position better than our other personnel. Some teams prefer to place a forward in the baseline position because of his size and his ability to guard the ball under the goal and in the corners, making it extremely difficult to shoot over him because of his height and defensive range. We have used a forward on the baseline in the past, but prefer to utilize a guard in the baseline position and sacrifice height and defensive range for the speed and defensive alertness and anticipation that most guards possess. Also, keep in mind that the baseline man must cover the corners, thus taking him away from the boards and rebounding opportunities. By playing a guard on the baseline, we are not sacrificing any rebounding strength and can cover the boards with our center and two forwards.

The following are the defensive rules that govern 2, the baseline man. He must realize the importance of them and his floor position.

Whenever the ball is out front he should play high and in front of any offensive player positioned on the block (Diagram 6-15).

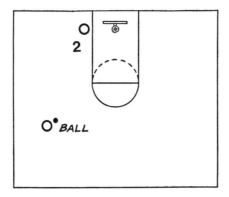

Diagram 6-15

Note: He is responsible for any lob pass to any player under the goal on the ball side of the floor.

As mentioned earlier, 2, whenever the ball is at the free-throw line extended or above it, must maintain a position with his inside foot slightly inside the lane area. He must do a good job anticipating a pass to the baseline corner area. If a pass is made to the baseline corner area, 2 must anticipate and react upon the flight of the ball. The instant the ball has left the passer's hand, 2 should be moving to cover the corner area (Diagram 6-16).

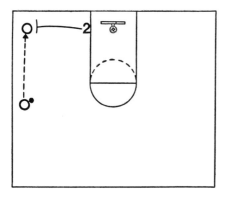

Diagram 6-16

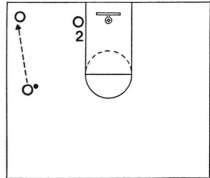

Diagram 6-17

Note: 2's approach to the ball is extremely important. He should take the first step toward the corner with the sideline foot, then quickly slide the inside foot in front making the approach with the sideline foot or baseline foot back, thus protecting the baseline. We instruct our baseline man to think "inside out" whenever making a corner approach. By this we mean that we apply pressure to the ball in the corner from inside (the baseline), influencing the ball to the middle, thus preventing the baseline drive.

This defensive maneuver, in some instances, is extremely difficult to execute, especially against teams that attempt to screen 2, the baseline man. 2 is instructed to play on the top side of all low post players (players positioned on the block). (Diagram 6-17.)

2, playing on top of the offensive player on the block, on the flight of the ball reacts to the corner, moving with his sideline foot first toward the baseline, and makes his defensive approach from the baseline. Again, remember our teaching terminology "Inside Out." (Diagram 6-18).

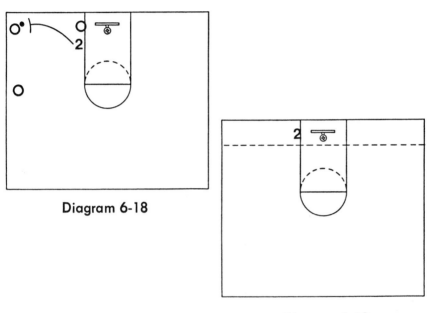

Diagram 6-18

Diagram 6-19

Note: This defensive maneuver is a looping one, as 2 cannot make a straight line defensive approach without giving up the baseline.

It is imperative that pressure be placed on the ball from out front by the point and the wing men. If pressure is not on the ball out front, then 2's baseline position is very vulnerable to a lob pass to a big man underneath.

2, whenever the ball is at the free-throw line extended or above it, should maintain a position on the baseline with his inside foot just inside the lane area and his sideline foot extended toward the corner. His weight should be placed on his sideline foot to allow him quicker movement to cover the corner area.

The defensive floor coverage area that 2 is responsible for is illustrated in Diagram 6-19.

Note: You will see that 2 is responsible for the entire baseline. He must possess exceptional lateral movement to cover both corners of the baseline.

THE 1-3-1 ZONE DEFENSIVE SLIDES
AGAINST OFFENSIVE ATTACKS

Many teams will attack the 1-3-1 zone defense with a two-guard offensive front, the theory being to create a two-on-one situation on the defensive point man (Diagram 6-20).

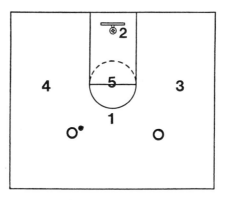

Diagram 6-20

It is imperative that the wing man on the ball side (either 3 or 4) and 5, the post man, come up quickly to stop penetration. The wing man must maintain his defensive body angle to prevent a direct pass to the baseline. When one of the offensive guards attempt to penetrate, Diagram 6-21, 1, 4 and 5 must come up quickly and stop penetration, and pressure the ball aggressively. As mentioned earlier, we triple-team the ball when first penetrated, then release on the flight of the ball. The only passes that the offensive player should be able to complete are the bounce pass or lob pass.

Note: 3, the right wing man, drops halfway to the basket, with his weight on his inside foot toward the block or basket to prevent a lay-up. 2, the baseline man, plays high on the ball side, fronting any offensive player in his defensive area.

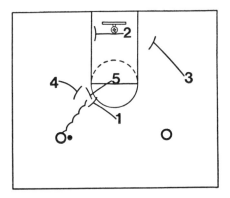

Diagram 6-21

We will now discuss the defensive coverage of the 1-3-1 zone defense with the ball in the baseline corner area. This is an extremely vulnerable area of the 1-3-1 zone and the defensive responsibilities of each player must be executed perfectly.

Diagram 6-22 shows the ball in the baseline corner area.

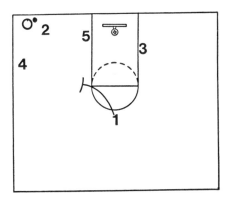

Diagram 6-22

2, the baseline man, is pressuring the ball while protecting the baseline area. 4, the left wing man, has positioned himself in the passing lane between the offensive man in the corner and the offensive guard on the ball side of the floor.

4's responsibilities are two-fold: he must prevent any direct pass back out to the offensive guard; and also help prevent penetration in the event the offensive man attempts to penetrate from the corner area.

5, the center, has quickly slid down the lane and protected the block or the basket area. He must front and prevent any pass from coming inside to the low lane area that 2 had covered before releasing and going to the corner.

1, the defensive point man or monster man, must quickly drop to the side of the free-throw-lane area and as deep as one step below, according to the pressure being applied to the ball and the movement of the offensive player into the high post area.

3, the right wing man, has dropped halfway to the block to protect the basket area. An exception can be made when, with the ball in the corner area, the passing angle across the baseline to under the basket area is poor. 3 should place his weight on his front foot, enabling him to react quicker to a diagonal pass from the corner across the floor to the offensive guard opposite the ball (Diagram 6-23).

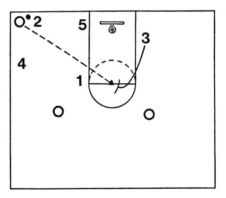

Diagram 6-23

Note: In this particular situation with the ball in the corner, we encourage 3, who is our quickest forward, to anticipate this pass and attempt the interception.

Another defensive coverage that we utilize when the ball is in the corner on the baseline is the "wing-sag." The wing man, instead of taking a position in the passing lane between the offensive player on the baseline and the offensive guard, quickly sags toward the high and medium lane area (Diagram 6-24).

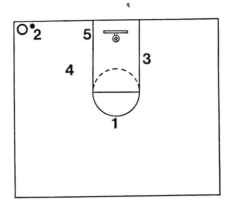

Diagram 6-24

All other defensive players have the same defensive responsibilities, except, 1, the defensive point man or monster man. 1 must play high and prevent any direct guard-to-guard pass or direct pass to the opposite side of the floor.

Diagram 6-25 illustrates the wing-sag maneuver, with the ball passed back outside and 1, the point man, positioning himself high in the passing lane to prevent a direct pass from guard to guard.

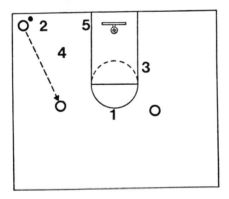

Diagram 6-25

Note: Wing men 4 and 3 should coordinate their defensive slides with 1, the point man, whenever the ball is in the corner of the baseline and the wing man on the ball side positions himself in the passing lane. 1, the point man, sags to protect the high post area.

In the event the wing man executes a wing-sag maneuver, then 1, the point man, must come high and position himself in the passing lane to prevent a direct pass to the opposite side of the floor.

We instruct our wing man to play the passing lane when we first apply the 1-3-1 zone and then, as the offense starts to adjust, we want them to vary their defensive coverage, utilizing the wing-sag and the passing lane defensive positioning.

It is important that the ball is pressured and the offensive player is prevented from making a direct pass to the opposite side of the floor.

Another important defensive coverage of the 1-3-1 zone is when the ball is passed into the post.

Whenever the ball is passed to an offensive player inside from the corner or wing positions, we will double-team the ball with 5, the center, applying high pressure on the ball and 2, the baseline man, applying quick pressure from his baseline position (Diagram 6-26).

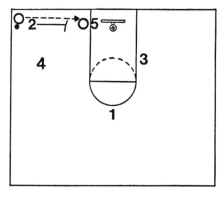

Diagram 6-26

Note: We refer to this double-team maneuver as "stripping down" and we do not want to allow the inside offensive player to shoot or to make a direct pass out to a teammate. If he passes out to a teammate, the passes should be limited to either a bounce pass or a lob pass.

We will also double-team with 1, the point man, if the ball is passed into the high post area from out front. 1 should react quickly upon the flight of the ball and double-team the ball (Diagram 6-27).

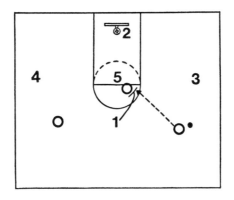

Diagram 6-27

THE 1-3-1 ZONE VERSUS THE
DOUBLE LOW POST

This offensive set is a very popular way to attack the 1-3-1 zone defense, positioning an offensive player on each block underneath the basket (Diagram 6-28).

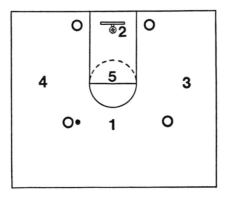

Diagram 6-28

Whenever we encounter a team employing an offensive set with a double low post, we will adjust our 1-3-1 zone defense to neutralize this offensive alignment. We will tighten our wing men 3 and 4, positioning them closer to the lane area. This protects the lane area from a direct pass from a guard to the block area. We will also vary 5, the post man's, defensive coverage. He will not come high to stop offensive penetration but will float in the lane area and help protect. Whenever this occurs, the wing men 3 and 4 and 1, the point man, must do a good job of stopping offensive penetration from out front (Diagram 6-29).

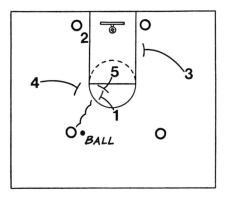

Diagram 6-29

Note: Against the double low offensive attack, we will double-team offensive penetration from out front instead of the regular triple-team.

THE 1-3-1 ZONE DEFENSE VERSUS
THE 1-4 OFFENSIVE ATTACK

The 1-4 offensive attack is one of the most successful attacks used against zone defenses. This unusual offensive alignment has been an enigma to the zone defense and presents it with coverage problems. Diagram 6-30, illustrates the 1-4 offensive alignment against the 1-3-1 zone defense.

We adjust the defensive coverage on our 1-3-1 zone to counteract the 1-4 offensive alignment.

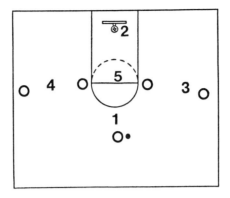

Diagram 6-30

The key to the defensive coverage against the 1-4 offensive alignment is 1, the point man's, aggressive pressure on the ball. 1 must pressure the ball and keep the ball isolated on one side of the floor. He must not allow the offensive point man to change sides of the floor and reverse with the ball (Diagram 6-31).

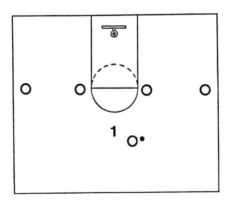

Diagram 6-31

Note: 1 should come out and attack the dribbler influencing him to one side of the floor and isolating the ball on one side of the floor.

The defensive responsibilities of the other players are illustrated in Diagram 6-32.

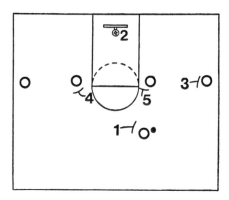

Diagram 6-32

3, the right wing, pressures the ball-side offensive wing man. 5, the post man, fronts the offensive post man on the ball-side of the floor. 4, the left wing man, moves in and fronts or plays inside of the other offensive post man. He must be alert for a quick pass from the offensive point man. 2, the baseline man, maintains his position in the lane, but he should play in the middle of the lane and be alert for any lob passes to the post men. Since 4 and 5 are fronting the offensive post man, 2 must protect against the lob pass.

Chapter 7

Defensive Stunts from the
1-3-1 Zone Defense

The zone defense in basketball during recent years has undergone many rejuvenations and changes. The zone defenses of today, unlike the zone defenses utilized in years past, have constantly adjusted to the offensive movement of the players and the ball. The trend in defensive basketball today is going away from the standard or straight zone defense, and a team playing a straight zone defense without utilizing defensive stunts runs the risk of allowing an offensive team to tear their defense to shreds. Defensive stunts with zone defenses are being utilized today more than ever before, and with great success. The reason for their success is mainly due to the stereotyped pattern offenses used to attack zone defenses. By combining defensive stunts with zone defenses, a team will be able to completely disrupt the offensive rhythm of an offensive team attempting to attack the zone defense. Also, the tremendous improvement in the offensive basketball player of today, especially in the areas of shooting and passing, has helped to bring about this trend in zone defenses and forced teams playing straight zone defenses to stunt with their defenses and vary their coverages.

It is important to note, however, that the defensive stunts which we will discuss in this chapter will be more effective if used for short periods of time. The defensive stunts that we utilize with our 1-3-1 zone defense, have proved to be extremely effective for short periods of time. We will in many instances stunt our 1-3-1 zone for a while, then play our straight 1-3-1 zone and then go back to our 1-3-1 zone defensive stunts again. This method of utilizing defensive stunts by alternating them off and on over periods of time has added to their effectiveness and brought confusion to our opposition.

Another extremely important point that we would like to emphasize is that the man-to-man is our basic defense and the 1-3-1 zone defense with defensive stunts is our secondary defense. We usually drill every day in practice on basic defensive fundamentals.

We utilize these defensive drills both in pre-season and during the year in our practices. We feel that this constant repetition of basic defensive fundamentals will reinforce our defense. In many instances, teams that utilize stunting defenses are not sound fundamentally, due to the fact that they do not work on defensive fundamentals every day in their practice sessions.

Our scouting reports help us determine what defensive stunts we will use against an opponent. They also give us an indication as to the length or period of time we can utilize the stunts before we start to alternate them. A good scouting report is extremely important to any team that relies on stunting defenses.

Many basketball teams that utilize defensive stunts with their zone have tendencies not to be aggressive. Coaches feel there is a certain correlation between stunting defenses and non-aggressive or passive defenses. We have counteracted this tendency with the full-court, pressure man-to-man defense. Let me explain that whenever we are going to stunt with our 1-3-1 zone against a team, we start the game in a full-court, man-to-man press for the first few minutes. We feel this helps to make our players aggressive and really get after our opponents. It makes them get their feet moving and places them in an aggressive frame of mind.

We are now going to illustrate and discuss the defensive stunts we utilize with our 1-3-1 zone defense. These stunts have been successful for us and have been responsible for many victories, helping us to stymie our opposition for short periods of time, thus enabling us to defeat them.

The following is our defensive alignment whenever we are going to stunt from our 1-3-1 zone defense (Diagram 7-1).

You will notice that the initial defensive alignment of our 1-3-1

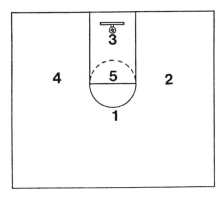

Diagram 7-1

zone whenever we are going to stunt is different from that of our regular 1-3-1 zone defense. The difference is that whenever we play our regular 1-3-1 zone defense, we play 2, a guard, on the baseline and whenever we are stunting with the 1-3-1 zone we play 3, our quick forward, on the baseline. The 1, 4 and 5 set up in the same initial positions in both zone coverages.

THE "FLEX" STUNT

Many offensive teams we encounter when using our 1-3-1 zone will attempt to penetrate the gaps in our 1-3-1 zone and then pass the ball down on the baseline for the shot. Against offensive teams that have two good, quick guards who can penetrate our zone and hurt us, we will utilize the "flex" stunt to counteract this offensive penetration.

Diagram 7-2 illustrates an offensive team attempting to attack our 1-3-1 zone with two offensive guards penetrating the gaps of our 1-3-1 zone defense.

To counteract this offensive penetration, we utilize the "flex" stunt. 1, the defensive point man, is the key to the success of the flex stunt. 1 signals the stunt with a visual signal to his teammate (we have used a clinched fist, open palm, etc.) when the offensive guard with the ball maneuvers into an attack position on the floor. The 1-3-1 zone rotates clockwise and matches up with the offensive alignment. 1 and 2

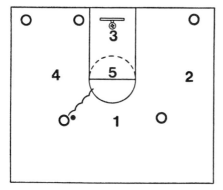

Diagram 7-2

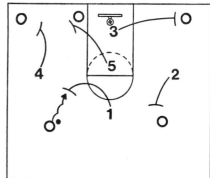

Diagram 7-3

play the offensive guards attempting to penetrate our zone nose-to-nose, positioning their bodies directly in front of the offensive guards. This takes away the gaps that the offensive guards were attempting to penetrate (Diagram 7-3).

Note: This defensive rotation with 2, the initial defensive wing man, rotating up and out into a defensive guard position, brings 3, the initial baseline man, out to the vacated wing position of 2 and he will pick up the offensive forward in that area. 5 will pick up the interior post man at whatever position he may be set up inside.

The flex stunt enables us to rotate into either a 2-3 zone defense or a man-to-man defense.

Diagram 7-4, illustrates the tight 2-3 zone defensive alignment.

The 2-3 zone can be either a tight zone or a pressure-laning-type zone, depending upon the personnel and the coach's defensive philosophy.

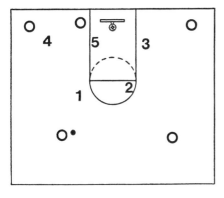

Diagram 7-4

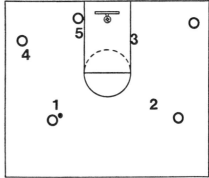

Diagram 7-5

Diagram 7-5, illustrates the pressure man-to-man defense that we can rotate into with the flex stunt.

In many instances, we have flexed out our 1-3-1 zone into a pressure man-to-man defense and attacked the offense. This element of surprise caused by placing good pressure on the ball and overplaying the passing lanes has caught several offensive teams off balance and enabled us to spurt to a victory.

THE "PIVOT" STUNT

The "Pivot" stunt is a simple defensive move that we have incorporated to add to the effectiveness of our 1-3-1 zone defense. Many teams, after playing against our 1-3-1 zone, will attempt to attack it with a double low post as illustrated in Diagram 7-6.

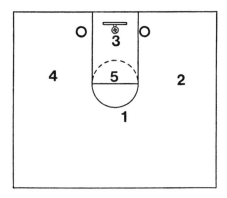

Diagram 7-6

Note: The double low offensive alignment is an excellent method of attacking the 1-3-1 zone defense, as it affords the offense a two-on-one situation on the baseline.

Whenever a team is hurting our 1-3-1 zone defense with the double low offensive alignment, we will utilize the pivot stunt. In executing the pivot stunt, 5 slides low to the baseline on the left side of the lane, 3 slides across to the right side of the lane and we are now in a 1-2-2 zone defense (Diagram 7-7).

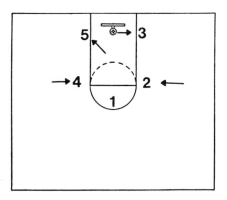

Diagram 7-7

Note: It is important to note that 1, 2, and 4, will tighten up the zone by moving toward the lane area. We play the 1-2-2 zone defense tight to eliminate the offensive inside attack.

We will usually key the pivot stunt from the bench with a visual key to 5, the post man. The remaining players will react to 5's movement to the baseline and slide into 1-2-2 zone defensive positions.

THE "DIAMOND AND ONE" STUNT

The "Diamond and One" stunt is one that we have used against teams which rely basically on one outside shooter against zone defenses. The 1-3-1 zone and the Diamond and One stunt blend in well with each other. We will play the 1-3-1 zone and then change to the Diamond and One stunt, alternating these two defenses as the situation calls for.

Diagram 7-8, illustrates the 1-3-1 zone defensive floor positions before we stunt.

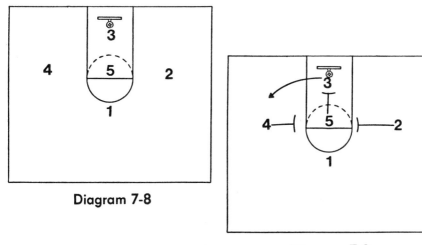

Diagram 7-8

Diagram 7-9

Note: When we employ the Diamond and One stunt, if the offensive player whom we will defend man-to-man with a chaser is an offensive forward, then we will place 3, our quick forward, on the baseline as we do whenever we utilize our defensive stunts.

Diagram 7-9 illustrates the defensive rotation we utilize in stunting from the 1-3-1 zone into a Diamond and One defense.

3, the baseline defensive man, comes out quickly and plays the high scoring offensive forward or wing man man-to-man defensively. 5, the center, moves down the lane and becomes the baseline man in the diamond zone, 4 and 2 move toward the lane area and tighten up the wings of the zone. 1, the defensive point man, drops back to protect the high lane area. We instruct 1 to establish his position with his inside foot touching the top of the key area. Diagram 7-10 illustrates how the "Diamond and One" defense looks after we have rotated into it.

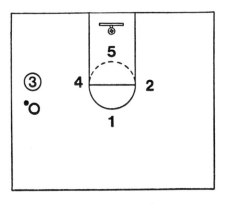

Diagram 7-10

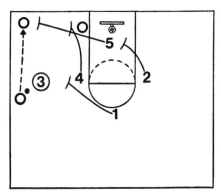

Diagram 7-11

Note: The defensive coverage of the diamond zone as follows: 5, the baseline man on the diamond, is responsible for coverage of the baseline area from corner to corner. The only time he does not cover the corner area is when the offensive player the chaser is guarding is in the corner. Diagram 7-11 shows 5, covering the corner area of the baseline and the defensive slides of the diamond zone.

5 covers the corner area pressuring the basketball, 4, the wing man on the ball side, upon seeing 5 leave the lane area to cover the corner area, quickly slides down the lane and defends the block on the low post area under the basket. 1, the point man, sags in toward the ball side and defends the high-to-medium post area. 2, the offside wing man slides down halfway and defends the offside block area and the offside wing area.

The defensive coverage is different if 5 has to defend the corner area when 3, the chaser, is on the opposite side of the floor. The defensive coverage in this situation must be adjusted as the wing area is open since 3, the chaser, is on the opposite side of the floor. Diagram 7-12, illustrates the defensive coverage whenever the chaser is in the corner on the opposite side of the ball.

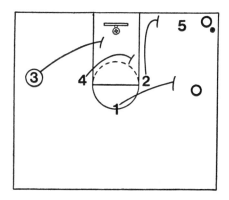

Diagram 7-12

5 is pressuring the ball in the corner and 2, the wing man, quickly rolls low and fronts any player in the low post area. These slides are the same as before. 1, the defensive point man, must alter his defensive coverage and rotate out to the open wing area and defend against any offensive player in that area. 4, the defensive wing man on the opposite side of the floor, quickly moves across and assumes the defensive responsibilities of the defensive point position. He defends the high and medium post areas of the zone defense. 3, the chaser, sags off of his man and protects the back-side area of the zone and is alert for possible lob passes to the low post and the lane area.

If the offensive player we want to play man-to-man coverage

on with a chaser is a guard, then we will alter our initial 1-3-1 alignment. We will place a guard on the baseline initially instead of a forward (Diagram 7-13).

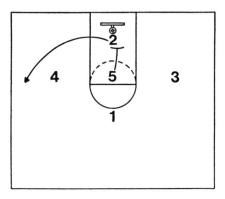

Diagram 7-13

2 has rotated out to man-to-man coverage and the diamond zone and defensive floor alignment would look as illustrated in Diagram 7-14.

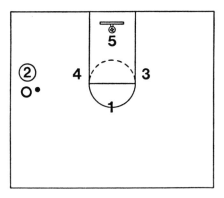

Diagram 7-14

The Diamond and One Stunt combined with the 1-3-1 zone can be devastatingly effective against a team that relies on one outside shooter against a zone defense. Alternating and changing those defenses and not giving the offensive team a chance to adjust to them can completely upset a team's offensive attack.

THE "CUTTER COVERAGE" STUNT

Many teams will attempt to attack our 1-3-1 zone defense by sending a cutter through to the baseline. They also utilize the offensive maneuver of sending a cutter, usually a guard, to the baseline to determine whether the defense they are facing is a zone or a man-to-man. We will utilize the "Cutter Coverage" stunt against many of our opponents who send their guards through to the baseline. The "Cutter Coverage" stunt is an excellent method of defending against this particular offensive maneuver, since in many instances it will not only defend against this particular offensive maneuver, but it will confuse the offensive team.

Diagram 7-15 illustrates an offensive team sending a cutter through our 1-3-1 zone defense to the baseline.

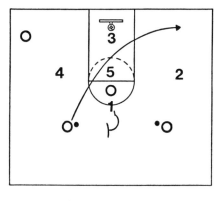

Diagram 7-15

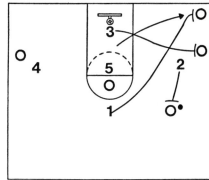

Diagram 7-16

Unless predetermined before the game by the scouting report, we will signal the Cutter Coverage stunt with a closed fist. 1, the point man on our 1-3-1 zone, will visually signal for the Cutter Coverage Stunt. 1 will then follow the cutter through to the baseline as shown in Diagram 7-16.

After 1 has followed the offensive cutter through to the baseline, 2 will rotate up and assume the defensive point position. 3, the baseline man, will rotate out to the wing and fill the wing position that 2 has just vacated. We will use the same defensive rotation, regardless of which corner the offensive guard cuts to, as we always want 2 to rotate up to the defensive point position.

Diagram 7-17, illustrates the offensive cutter moving into the opposite corner.

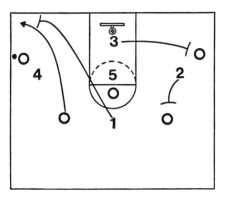

Diagram 7-17

Note: By maintaining the same defensive rotation, regardless of the corner the cutter goes to, we can always have a guard on the point of our 1-3-1 zone defense and without taking a rebounder off the boards.

After our defensive rotation, we can match-up with the offensive team and play them a man-to-man defense. We can also stay in our 1-3-1 zone defense and allow 1 to become the defensive baseline man and 2 the defensive point man. Against teams that send the guard through and quickly bring him back outside, we will have 1 follow him through and then follow him back outside again and we are automatically back in our 1-3-1 zone defense.

THE "BASELINE RULE" STUNT

The "Baseline Rule" stunt is similar to that of the cutter coverage stunt. Many teams will attack zone defenses from the baseline area and will attempt to get the ball to the baseline initially against zone defenses. Our scouting report will play an important part in determining whether we will put the Baseline Rule stunt into effect or not. The rule is that any time the ball is on the baseline, we are automatically in man-to-man coverage against all offensive cutters.

Diagram 7-18 illustrates the ball being passed to the baseline against our 1-3-1 zone defense and a wing cutter going through.

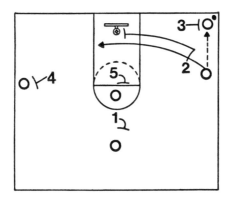

Diagram 7-18

After the baseline rule has been put in effect and the ball is passed back outside, we can stay in a man-to-man defense coverage or we can shift back into a zone defense. If we go back into a zone defense, it will be a 1-3-1 zone defense with 2 on the baseline and 3 rotating up to the wing position.

Chapter 8

The 1-3-1 Zone
Trapping Defense

The constantly changing game of basketball has undergone many changes in the last decade. It has placed more emphasis than ever before on quickness and reaction, especially in the area of team defense. The trend today in basketball is the utilization of trapping defenses. It is our feeling that if a team has a good trapping defense, it will always be in the game and will often rally from a large point deficit to a victory.

At Middle Tennessee State University, our basketball program places major emphasis on the fast break, an exciting, aggressive type of play that the players and most fans enjoy. The 1-3-1 zone trapping defense we have utilized has complemented this style of play and enabled us to apply pressure to our opponents on both ends of the floor.

The 1-3-1 zone trapping defense can be adjustable to many situations. It offers a team an excellent method to upset an opponent early in a game or it can be held back until that critical moment late in a game when the team needs to gain the momentum in order to gain a victory.

The following are some very important points to consider in coaching the 1-3-1 trapping defense. The effective 1-3-1 trapping defense is not easily taught and a coach should not become disappointed with inadequate early defensive execution by his players. Patience is the key to coaching and teaching this defense. Through repetition of their defensive responsibilities and slides, the players will eventually become extremely competent. In most instances, players like the trapping defense, will exert extra effort and will become extremely aggressive in executing it. It is of extreme importance to the success of the 1-3-1 zone trapping defense that the players exert an all-out effort for the duration of the defense.

Before diagramming and illustrating the 1-3-1 zone trapping defense, let us briefly discuss some of its positive attributes. (1) Players like to play the aggressive style of defensive trapping basketball and they take great pride in their aggressive play. (2) The all important tempo control of a game can be dictated by this aggressive style of play. (3) It forces a team out of their shooting range and encourages them to take bad shots. (4) It promotes a fast-breaking style of offensive play. (5) It enables a team to steal the ball by applying pressure to the ball and also by showing passing lanes that look to be open but are not. (6) It is capable of completely neutralizing a screening, pattern-oriented type team. (7) It forces turnovers by the offensive team in attempting to attack it. (8) When behind, a team must gain the advantage both defensively and offensively, therefore, the trapping defense affords every team an opportunity to come from behind. (9) It forces opposing coaches to spend a large amount of their practice time preparing to combat the 1-3-1 zone trapping defense. (10) The 1-3-1 zone trapping defense affords a team good basket protection, always creating a tandem defense in front of the ball and the basket.

Let us now illustrate and discuss this defense in detail.

THE 1-3-1 ZONE TRAPPING DEFENSE

The 1-3-1 zone trap is a sound defense designed to apply defensive pressure to the offensive team, forcing them into turnovers and mistakes. It is important to emphasize that we do not attempt to steal the ball every time, but try to force the offense into making other types of mistakes.

Diagram 8-1 illustrates the defensive alignment of the 1-3-1 zone trapping defense.

Note: Our numbering system is the same as in our straight 1-3-1 zone defense.

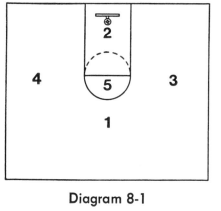

Diagram 8-1

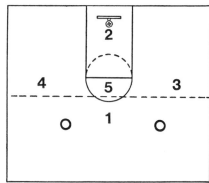

Diagram 8-2

In executing our 1-3-1 zone trapping defense, the point man 1 plays between the top of the key and the mid-court circle. He will vary his initial defensive position, usually meeting the offensive line of attack closer to the mid-court circle. 1, the point man's, primary defensive responsibility is to force the dribble by the offensive guard with the ball. 1 forces the ball to one side of the floor; this will determine the strong side (ball side) and the weak side. 1 will force the ball to the side of the floor of the weakest offensive player or the toughest defensive player, depending on the scouting report and the game plan. It is important that a team establish its penetration line (this will vary, depending upon the coach).

Against teams utilizing two-guard fronts, we do not want the guards to penetrate deeper than an imaginary line between the top of the key and the free-throw line.

It is important to the success of the 1-3-1 zone trapping defense that 1 prevents any direct guard-to-guard pass. By this we mean any pass other than a lob or a bounce pass (Diagram 8-2).

Note: In coaching terminology we refer to this pass as the "Ping-Pong" pass. A guard-to-guard pass changes the defensive responsibilities of the defensive players, therefore, we want to isolate the ball on one side of the floor if possible.

It is also extremely important to emphasize that the defensive players executing the defensive traps always move under control. They should not play with reckless abandon, but should always maintain good body control, thereby creating good double-teams and passing lane coverage.

Defensive wing men 3 and 4 set up their initial defensive position dependent upon the point man's initial defensive position. In most instances, they will set up between the free-throw line extended and the top of the key (Diagram 8-3).

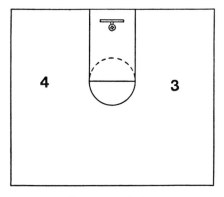

Diagram 8-3

The wing man on the ball side of the floor, who will be executing the double-team with the point man, must use good timing. His double-team area will be dependent upon the point man's floor position. However, when executing his double-teams, he should not double-team too quickly as this will leave a large floor area on the backline open.

5, the defensive post man's, initial floor position is in the high key area. He fronts any offensive player in that area and must be constantly alert for offensive players flashing into the "seam" of the 1-3-1 zone trap. 5 must stay between the ball and the goal at all times. The ball should never be handled at the high post. A good rule of thumb for 5 to follow is that when the ball is out front, he should never be lower than the free-throw line and never higher than the top of the key.

The defensive baseline man's, 2, initial floor position again is dependent upon the point man's alignment. However, he should set up between the broken lines of the free-throw circle and the basket. When the ball is out front, 2 should be on the ball side of the lane area with his inside foot in the lane.

Diagram 8-4, illustrates the initial defensive floor alignment of 5, the post man, and 2, the baseline man.

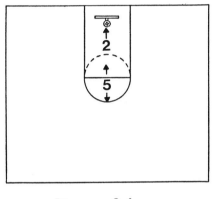

Diagram 8-4

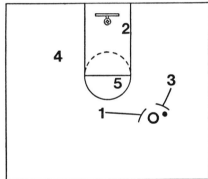

Diagram 8-5

Note: It is important that 5 and 2 always be in position between the ball and the basket whenever the ball is out front.

Now that we have discussed the basic defensive player positions and defensive responsibilities of the 1-3-1 trapping defense, let us discuss the defensive trapping situations.

Diagram 8-5 illustrates a defensive trapping situation on an offensive guard out front with 1, the point man, and 3, the right wing man. We will first discuss the execution of the double-team and discuss all other players' defensive responsibilities in relationship to the double-team.

1, the point man, and 3, the wing man, execute an aggressive double-team on the offensive guard. The double-team is formed intelligently without reaching or fouling. 1 and 3 keep their hands up and their feet constantly moving. 3 closes the double-team with 1 taking away the passing lane to the baseline with a good defensive body angle on the ball. 1 and 3 in their defensive positions should play square on the ball. Unlike the basic 1-3-1 zone, 5 does not react to stop offensive penetration. Instead, he plays high and as always between the ball and the goal. (We will allow him to float and have freedom in his movement, but he must always have the hand closest to the double-team between the ball and the basket.) (Diagram 8-6.)

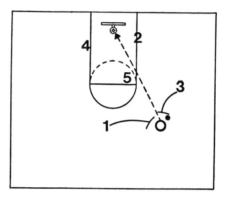

Diagram 8-6

1 and 3 in executing the double-team must form it quickly and not allow the offensive guard to split them. 3's primary responsibility is to stop penetration by the offensive guard. Ideally, his inside foot should split the offensive guard's body. 1 reacting at the same time is the "seal" man. He moves in and closes the double-team, placing his inside foot close to 3's and applying strong lateral pressure to the ball. 2, the baseline man, maintains his defensive position on the ball side of the lane, constantly alert for a pass to the baseline on the ball side of the floor or a diagonal pass. 4, the opposite wing man, drops slightly to the baseline to protect the back-side area, but with his weight on his front foot always ready to make the quick move back outside.

The most common offensive attack against the 1-3-1 trap is with a two-guard offensive front. One offensive guard with the ball will penetrate inviting the double-team and then pass to the opposite guard. Diagram 8-7, illustrates the defensive slides of the 1-3-1 trap in defending against the guard-to-guard pass.

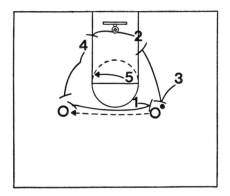

Diagram 8-7

    4, the opposite wing man, is the key to stopping this maneuver if they are successful in completing the guard-to-guard pass. 4 comes up quick and hard (under control) maintaining a good body angle and blocking the passing lane to the baseline (this is an important point as a quick pass to the baseline can create an open jump shot before 2, the baseline man, can recover). 1 comes across the floor on a square route; he must react quickly, applying pressure to the ball and clamping the double-team on the ball with 4. 5, the post man, comes straight across the lane (he does not go lower in the lane) getting between the ball and the goal. 2, the baseline man, moves across the lane to the ball side of the floor. 3, now the opposite wing man, drops back to protect the block and back-side area.

    In the event that a good double-team or trap is formed out front. we instruct the three players not involved in the trap to watch the passer (in most instances his eyes). They will be able to react more quickly to the next pass by doing this and in many instances intercept cross-court lateral and diagonal passes. We allow 4 and 5 freedom of movement if a good double-team has been formed (the offensive player caught in the double-team or trap will only be able to throw a lob or bounce pass). The spacing of the offensive guards will, in most instances, determine who will be the interceptor of the guard-to-guard pass. If the offensive spacing is short, then 5 will use good judgment and go for the interception, if he knows he can get the ball (Diagram 8-8).

Note: 5's judgment in this situation is important. He should not gamble if there is any doubt in his mind. Once he commits, he must totally commit and go all the way.

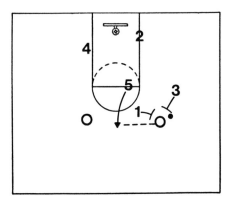

Diagram 8-8

Once 5 commits himself for the interception and he is not successful, we must quickly rotate defensively to recover and prevent the easy lay-up (Diagram 8-9).

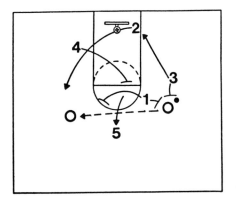

Diagram 8-9

4, the opposite wing man, quickly moves across to protect the vacated lane area. 2, the baseline man, quickly moves across and protects 4's vacated back-side area. If the ball is passed out of the double-team, 3 quickly drops back toward the basket area. 1, if the pass is completed to the other guard, quickly moves across to stop offensive penetration (Diagram 8-10).

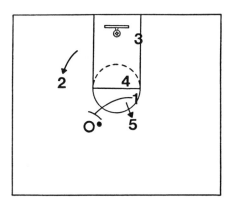

Diagram 8-10

After rotating to stop the offensive thrust or penetration after 5's attempting interception, 5, whose interception attempt has placed him out of position, quickly turns and fills the vacated right wing position. Diagram 8-11 illustrates the defensive recovery rotations.

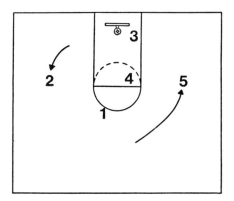

Diagram 8-11

2 moves up to the wing position, 3 replaces 2 on the baseline, 4 protects the lane area, 5 has filled the right wing and 1 remains at the

point position. *They maintain these positions and revert to a basic 1-3-1 zone defense. We do not double-team with our post man out of position on the wing.*

In the event that the offensive spacing of the offensive guards is wide and the guard-to-guard pass is lengthened, then 4, the opposite wing man, becomes the interceptor.

Diagram 8-12 illustrates the defensive double-team by 1 and 3 on the offensive guard out front. Note that the offensive spacing of the two offensive guards is wider than before.

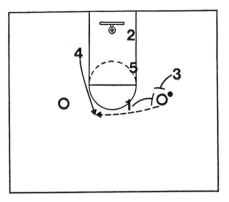

Diagram 8-12

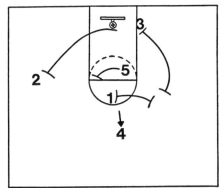

Diagram 8-13

Note: 4, upon seeing 1 and 3 execute a good defensive double-team, moves higher out on the floor and moves into an interceptor position. 4 must use good judgment and if the pass coming out of the double-team to the opposite offensive guard is a lob pass or a bounce pass, 4 should, in most instances, attempt the interception.

If 4's attempt to intercept the guard-to-guard pass is not successful, the defensive rotation is illustrated in Diagram 8-13.

2 moves out from the baseline and fills 4's vacated defensive wing position. 3 quickly moves from double-teaming the ball to the baseline, replacing 2. 1 and 5 assume their initial defensive responsibilities at the point and in the middle of the 1-3-1 trap.

An important point to remember is that if the offensive guard maintains his dribble during the double-team, he should be influenced or turned to the sidelines. The defensive wing man, after turning him to the sidelines, should then influence the ball to the corner if possible.

Many offensive teams attempt to attack the 1-3-1 trap by quickly passing the ball to the baseline area, the theory being to attempt to draw the double-team out front and then quickly passing the ball to the baseline for a quick jump shot (Diagram 8-14).

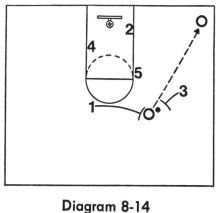

Diagram 8-14

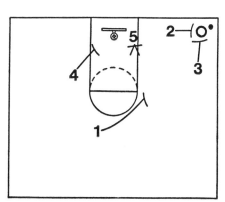

Diagram 8-15

2, the baseline man, upon seeing the ball being passed to the baseline moves out under control to pressure the ball. 2 must protect the block area until 5 can get down the lane to protect it. 2 approaches the ball from the baseline side (we refer to his approach as "inside out"). He applies pressure to the ball containing the offensive player until 3 can move down and help double-team. 3, the defensive wing man on the ball side, reacts quickly out of the initial double-team, moves to the baseline, blocking the passing lane, and executes a double-team with 2. 1, the defensive point man, plays between the ball and the middle of the free-throw line, adjusting to the offensive man along the lane area. 4 the opposite wing man, drops back and assumes a floor position halfway to the goal, anticipating a diagonal pass out of the double team (Diagram 8-15).

An excellent method of attacking the 1-3-1 zone trap is by the use of the diagonal pass. What we term the "Down and Out" pass can be extremely effective against the 1-3-1 zone trap. In executing the Down and Out pass, the offensive guard invites the double-team out front and passes the ball to the baseline. The offensive player on the baseline makes a quick diagonal pass across to the opposite side of the key.

Diagram 8-16, illustrates the Down and Out pass.

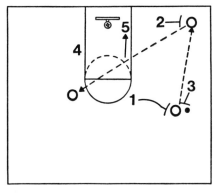

Diagram 8-16

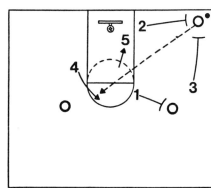

Diagram 8-17

Note: The diagonal pass out from the baseline, if quickly executed, can catch the 1-3-1 trap shifting and be thrown through the seam of the zone. The key to combating this offensive move is 4, the opposite wing man, who must keep his weight on the outside foot and be alert for the diagonal pass. In this situation, we encourage 4 to attempt the interception of the pass, as we want to keep the offense cautious about making the quick diagonal pass.

Diagram 8-17 shows 4, the opposite wing man, intercepting the Down and Out diagonal pass.

Note: The pass is being thrown in the seam of the 1-3-1 trap with 1 and 3 in the process of shifting defensive responsibilities. We work against this offensive attack daily in our practice sessions and prepare our players to defend against it.

Whenever the ball is passed from the baseline back outside to the ball-side guard, we recover defensively in the following manner. 1, the defensive point man, isolates the ball on one side of the floor; he does not allow a guard-to-guard pass. 3, the defensive wing man, quickly moves out playing in the passing lane to the baseline. 5, the defensive post man, moves up high quickly and positions himself between the ball and the basket. 2, the defensive baseline man, moves back to his initial defensive position on the ball side of the baseline. 4, the opposite wing man, moves into position protecting the block area, with his weight on his front foot ready to react to the free-throw line area (Diagram 8-18).

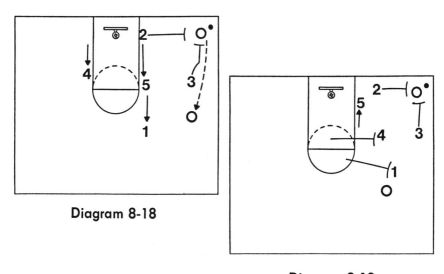

Diagram 8-18

Diagram 8-19

In the event that a good defensive double-team is formed on the baseline, we will stunt with our 1-3-1 trap. 4, the opposite wing man, must read or recognize that the ball is being well-double-teamed on the opposite baseline. On seeing this double-team, 4 verbally signals the defensive stunt by yelling the word "Blitz." The following is our defensive Blitz coverage (Diagram 8-19).

2, the defensive baseline man, double-teams the ball with 3 and blocks the driving and passing lane to the baseline. 3 double-teams the ball with 2 and blocks the passing lane out. 5, the defensive post man, positions between the ball and the basket. 1, the defensive point man, covers the outlet pass on the ball side of the double-team. 4, the opposite wing man, the key to the success of this stunt, flashes across and covers the middle of the lane area.

GENERAL TEAM DEFENSIVE RULES
FOR THE 1-3-1 ZONE TRAPPING DEFENSE

1. The players must be conditioned to watch the passer and react quickly.
2. Double-team intelligently—don't reach and foul—keep hands up and moving.
3. This defense must be played with "intensity." Pressure must be placed on the ball at all times.
4. Play aggressively, forcing the offense to make the mistakes.
5. Keep three defensive men positioned between the ball and the basket at all times.
6. Defensive players on the ball side of the floor should maintain good body angles in relation to the ball.

Chapter 9

Successful Drills to Develop the 1-3-1 Offensive and Defensive Systems

There are hundreds of drills that a basketball coach can utilize to help build and develop his offensive and defensive systems. The basketball coach of today can utilize drills to develop his players individually, both offensively and defensively, and also utilize drills to teach and develop his players and blend them into his offensive and defensive team concepts. We have analyzed the drills utilized over the years to develop our 1-3-1 offensive and defensive systems and condensed them into what we feel are the most essential ones.

OFFENSIVE DRILLS

The "Point Pressure" Drill

The "Point Pressure" drill is one we utilize to develop our offensive point man. This is an excellent drill that will over-simulate game-type man-to-man pressure which will be constantly applied to the offensive point man in the 1-3-1 offense.

The Point Pressure drill is divided into two different phases. Diagram 9-1 illustrates the initial positions of its first phase.

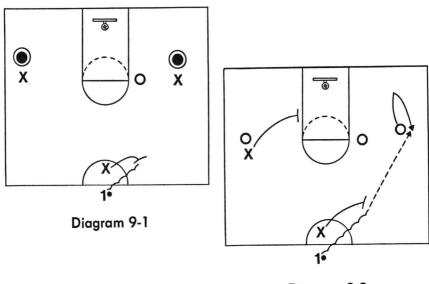

Diagram 9-1

Diagram 9-2

The alignment of the drill is as follows: 1, the offensive point man, has the basketball and his starting position is between the mid-court circle and the top of the key in the back-court area. A defensive player is also positioned there with 1. Two offensive wing men are positioned wide at the free-throw line extended with two defensive men overplaying them. An offensive post man sets up at a side high post position with no defensive man on him and has the freedom to move from side to side, depending upon the position of the basketball.

1, the offensive point man, must advance the ball by dribbling up the floor while being pressured and harassed by the defensive guard. 1 must penetrate with the ball into what we term the offensive "attack zone" and execute a crisp pass to one of the offensive wing men, who is being overplayed by a defensive forward. This requires coordinated movement and timing between the point man and the wing men.

Diagram 9-2 illustrates the successful execution of the point guard-to-wing man pass.

Note: The wing man, upon receiving the ball, "squares" up and faces the basket. 1, after passing to the wing man, either cuts to the basket or moves to the opposite side of the floor and sets a screen for the opposite wing man (Diagram 9-3).

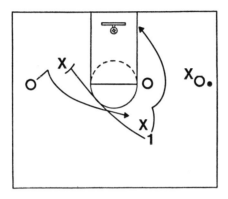

Diagram 9-3

In the event that the wing man is unable to free himself for the pass from the point man due to a strong defensive overplay at the wing position, the point man should attempt to bring the offensive wing man a step higher and quickly pass the ball to the unguarded high post man who executes a bounce pass to the wing man, who has cut to the basket for a backdoor lay-up (Diagram 9-4).

Note: In executing the backdoor cut, we instruct our wing men to come high to receive the ball, giving a passing target with the

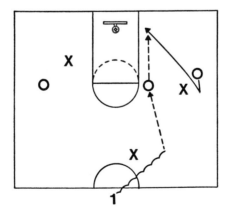

Diagram 9-4

sideline hand. Upon reading the defensive overplay, the wing man should push off the sideline foot and cut a deep baseline route to the basket.

The second phase of the Point Pressure drill is set up by adding a second defensive guard to the drill. The second defensive guard is positioned just behind the ten-second line, with all other positions of the drill, both offensively and defensively, the same. 1, the offensive point man, advances the ball up the floor while being pressured by the initial defensive guard. When he reaches mid-court, the initial defensive guard drops off and the second defensive guard quickly pressures the point man and attempts to turn him to the opposite side of the floor (Diagram 9-5).

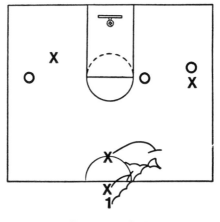

Diagram 9-5

Note: 1, the point man must stay under control at all times when executing against pressure. This phase of the drill is excellent for developing the point man's body control and floor awareness.

"Post Power" Drill

The "Post Power" drill is a drill we use to develop and coordinate the offensive movement of our interior post men. As discussed in Chapter 1, we designate our post men (interior players) as numbers 4 and 5. The drill is set up with 4 and 5 in crackdown floor positions, with defensive men guarding them. The coach is positioned at the point with the ball, two wing men are positioned on the wings with no defensive men guarding them.

The coach starts the drill by showing direction with the ball, 4 and 5 simulate crackdown screens and establish their high and low post (Diagram 9-6).

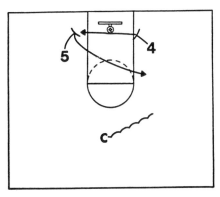

Diagram 9-6

The ball is passed around the perimeter and 4 and 5 work together to get open inside. The ball must be held by the perimeter people for a minimum of two seconds to allow 4 and 5 time to maneuver and work with each other.

Diagram's 9-7 to 9-9 illustrate the optional offensive movements of the post men.

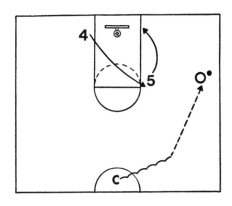

Diagram 9-7

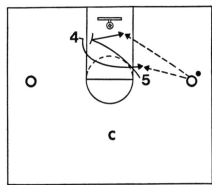

Diagram 9-8

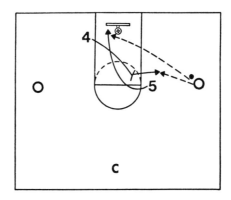

Diagram 9-9

Note: It is important to point out that the emphasis in this drill should be placed on constant communication between the post men 4 and 5. Another most important point is that we want to get the ball on the block at the low post position as often as possible. Quickness with the ball by the post men is extremely important; they should not hesitate—their initial moves should be quick.

Perimeter "Motion" Drill

This is an excellent drill involving the development of the three perimeter players 1, 2 and 3. The initial starter position of the perimeter "motion" drill has 1, the offensive point man, at the point position with a defensive man pressuring him. 2 and 3, the wing men, are set up at the offensive wing positions with defensive men pressuring them (Diagram 9-10).

1 initiates the drill by passing to either wing man 2 or 3. 1, after his pass, can cut to the basket, slide, screen opposite or replace himself. The same offensive rules apply in the motion offense. We stress good controlled movement with a purpose. We allow the offensive players to dribble only to drive to the basket, to improve their passing angle or if they are in trouble.

Diagrams 9-11 to 9-12 illustrate some of the offensive movement the drill encompasses.

Note: The coaching emphasis in this drill is placed upon offen-

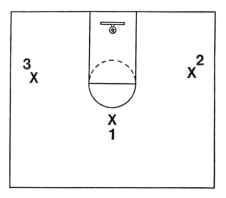

Diagram 9-10

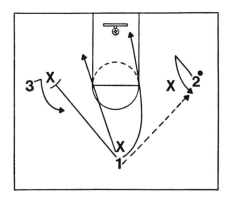

Diagram 9-11

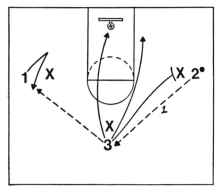

Diagram 9-12

sive movement without the ball: offensive wing men backdooring and clearing out when overplayed. All passes and cuts by the offensive players are "crisp" and well executed.

We have organized this drill into a competitive game. The initial offensive group has five possessions to attempt to score. The defensive group then converts to offense and has five possessions or attempts to score against the initial offensive group which has converted to defense. Each group has three series of five possessions totaling 15. The team that converts or scores the highest out of 15 possessions wins. Fouls are called against the defense and are counted as one point or one-half a basket. To add more competition to the drill, the losing group has to run sprints or "killer" drills.

Crackdown Drill

The crackdown drill helps to develop timing and offensive execution between the point man, wing men and post men, especially the interior timing between the post men and the wing men. The drill begins with all players involved set up to start on the ten-second line (Diagram 9-13).

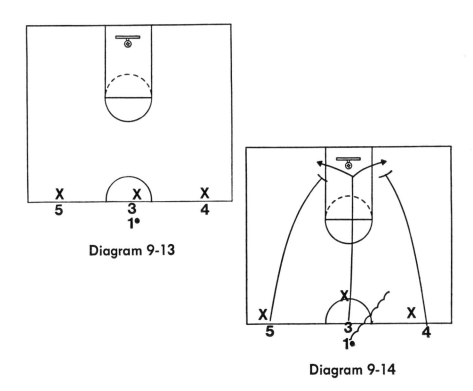

Diagram 9-13

Diagram 9-14

The players involved in the drill are 1, the offensive point man, with the ball and without any defensive player guarding him; 4 and 5, the post men, with two defensive men guarding them; 3, the wing man, with a defensive man to guard him. 3 sets up initially in the center of the court with 4 and 5 wide and 1 directly behind him with the ball.

1, who is set up about four to five steps behind the other players involved, begins the drill on the coach's whistle. 3 has the option of sprinting to either block in this drill and setting up; 4 and 5 sprint to their crackdown positions (Diagram 9-14).

4 and 5 must be alert as to the block where 3 positions himself. This is important as it dictates the offensive responsibilities of the post men. In the event 3 sets up on the block on 5's side of the floor, 5 must time his move with the offensive point man with the ball and execute a crackdown screen on 3 (Diagram 9-15).

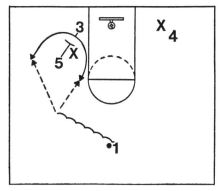

Diagram 9-15

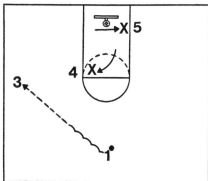

Diagram 9-16

Note: 3 should align himself for the crackdown screen by stepping deep into the lane before breaking off of 5's screen. If 3's defender overplays him to the outside, he should fake outside and break up the lane rubbing his defensive man off of 5's screen.

After the crackdown screen is executed and 1 passes to 3, the post men 4 and 5 begin their inside rotation. 5, after executing the crackdown screen, goes away from the ball to the opposite side of the lane while 4 flashes to the ball, thus establishing their high—low post identity (Diagram 9-16).

3 can pass to the post man flashing to the ball if he is open and when he receives the ball, the post men play a two-on-two game inside.

This drill is excellent for teaching and developing timing on the crackdown screens by the wing men and post men and for developing court awareness by the post men and the point guard.

Perimeter Split Drill

This is an offensive drill we utilize to develop the reactions and passing and splitting techniques of the perimeter players 1, 2 and 3. The perimeter players in the 1-3-1 offense must be alert to feed the post men at all times and after passing the ball into the post they must quickly react and execute a split with the closest perimeter player. This is an excellent drill to develop these offensive techniques.

The initial alignment of the drill places the three perimeter players 1, 2 and 3 at their offensive floor positions with defensive players guarding them. Offensive post men are positioned at a high side post position on each side of the lane without any defensive players guarding them (Diagram 9-17).

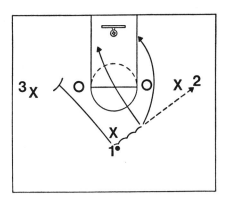

Diagram 9-17

1, the point man, has the ball and the drill begins with 1 passing the ball to either wing man 2 or 3. The offensive perimeter movement begins with 1's pass to 2 or 3. 1 can cut to the basket, rubbing his defensive man off on one of the stationary offensive post men, he can go away from the ball and set a screen, slide away from the ball or replace himself. It is important, as in previous drills, to stress good crisp passes and good movement without the ball by the perimeter players.

The perimeter players must make a minimum of three passes before they can pass to one of the post men. This rule is necessary and adds to the effectiveness of this drill as it makes the perimeter players pass and cut and force the defense to rotate before passing inside to the post men.

Diagram 9-18 shows 3, who has filled the point position after the initial offensive movement, passing the ball into a post man executing a split with 1 (Diagram 9-18).

3, after passing to the post man should move first as he makes the pass. 3 looks to screen 1's defensive man, 1 should take a dip step toward the baseline and cut off of 3's screen.

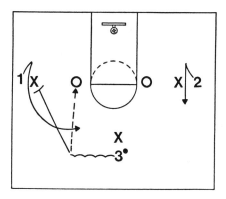

Diagram 9-18

Note: An important coaching point to emphasize is that the splits off of the post man should always be six feet away from the post man. (The reason is that in a game situation this gives the post man floor space enough to operate.)

Diagram 9-19 illustrates the ball being passed into the post man from 1 who has the ball at a wing position.

As stated earlier, the player who passes to the post man 1 moves first, setting a screen for 3.

This is a very versatile drill, but although we place emphasis on

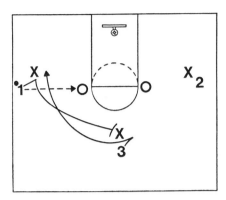

Diagram 9-19

the splitting situations, we encourage the perimeter players to back-door, clearout and allow controlled offensive freedom. The post man is to feed the open man and if a shot is not available and the ball is passed outside from a post man, the three-pass rule goes into effect again.

Competition is also added to this drill by allowing the initial offensive perimeter players five possessions in attempting to score. The offensive players then switch to defense and the defense to offense. Each group has a total of 15 possessions and the group converting the highest number of 15 offensive attempts wins. Fouls are called and are counted as one point or one-half a basket. Again the losing group has to run sprints or "killer" drills.

Half-Court—Full-Court Drill

This is an offensive drill that we utilize to work on both our set offensive attack and our full-court controlled breaking game. It is a unique drill in that it affords us the opportunity to work on two offensive attacks in a simulated game-type situation.

The drill starts in a team situation with five offensive players versus five defensive players. The offensive players or team execute their 1-3-1 offensive maneuvers against various man-to-man defensive coverages and zone defensive coverages (Diagram 9-20).

Note: We begin the drill with the offensive team in crackdown position ready to rotate into the 1-3-1 offensive alignment.

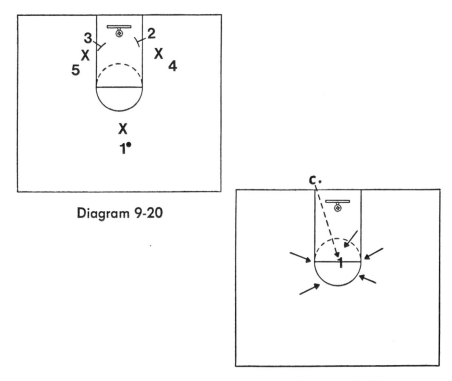

Diagram 9-20

Diagram 9-21

The offensive team does not take a shot while executing the 1-3-1 offensive maneuvers. They work on execution, timing and offensive reactions. This is the half-court phase or segment of the drill. We will now discuss the transition to the full-court phase of the drill. After the offense is in progress and several passes have been made with a lot of offensive movement, the coach, who is positioned underneath the goal holding a ball, blows the whistle. The offensive player with the ball, upon hearing the whistle, quickly throws the ball out of bounds, 1, the point guard, quickly sprints to the "bubble" or keyhole area and the coach passes the ball to him. (The defensive player guarding him does not try to intercept the pass.) (Diagram 9-21.)

Note: 1 must react quickly on the coach's whistle. He may be positioned on the wing, on the block, etc. How quick he is to react and receive the pass from the coach is the key to the full-court phase of this drill.

1 receives the pass from the coach. (We are now drilling on our 1-3-1 controlled breaking game.) 2 sprints down the floor to the block area, 4 sprints down and "posts" up on the block that 2 vacates when he moves out to the corner, 3 sprints to the opposite block and sets up. 5 sprints down and sets up at a crackdown position on the opposite side of the lane (Diagrams 9-22 and 9-23).

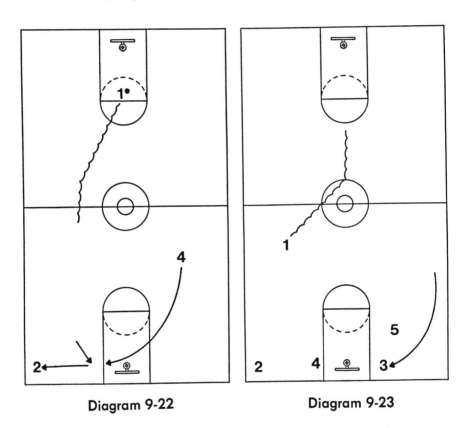

Diagram 9-22   Diagram 9-23

The offensive team executes all the offensive options in our transitional 1-3-1 breaking without taking a shot. On the coach's whistle, the ball is passed to the coach and the drill is started over again. This is an excellent offensive drill for timing, executing, etc. It is also an excellent conditioner and demands total offensive concentration.

Note: You can rotate teams, if you so desire, having the offensive team convert to defense and the defense to offense, or maintain the same offensive group the entire drill.

DEFENSIVE DRILLS

The Lateral Quickness Drill

The Lateral Quickness Drill is an excellent one that we utilize to improve our players' defensive movement. It is of extreme importance to the success of the zone defenses that the defensive players possess good lateral movement and quickness.

This drill is set up and begins with a defensive player positioned on the baseline in the center of the lane area (Diagram 9-24).

Note: The drill starts on the coach's whistle, with the coach positioned just beyond the top of the key with a stop watch.

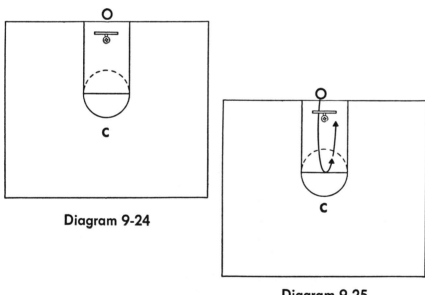

Diagram 9-24

Diagram 9-25

On the whistle, the player slides to the top of the key hole, in a staggered stance with his right foot extended, touching the top of the key hole with his right foot. After touching the top of the key, he executes a retreat step slide to an area just below the free-throw line extended (Diagram 9-25).

After reaching the lane area, the player slides as quickly as possible from side to side of the lane, touching the sides of the lane area (Diagram 9-26).

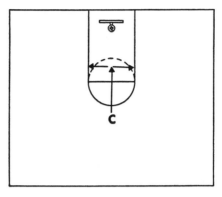

Diagram 9-26

Note: This drill is timed for 30 seconds and the number of lane touches each player can do is recorded by a manager.

This drill can be run at both ends of the floor. We divide the squad into two groups, the guards on one end and the forwards and centers on the other.

Defensive Reaction Drill

This is an excellent individual defensive reaction drill that can also be utilized as a conditioning drill. The drill begins by pairing the players off in groups of two's. Each pair should face each other across the mid-court line at about a six-foot spacing distance across and away from each other (Diagram 9-27).

Note: The coach who supervises the drill is stationed off at the side of the drill.

One line is designated by the coach as the "actors," the other line is the "reactors." Players in both lines assume a good defensive stance, the "actors" move in any direction, the reactors react quickly to the same defensive motion as that of the actors. The coach, during this drill, constantly stresses good defensive footwork. The defensive motion by the actors can be laterally or vertically. We also want the

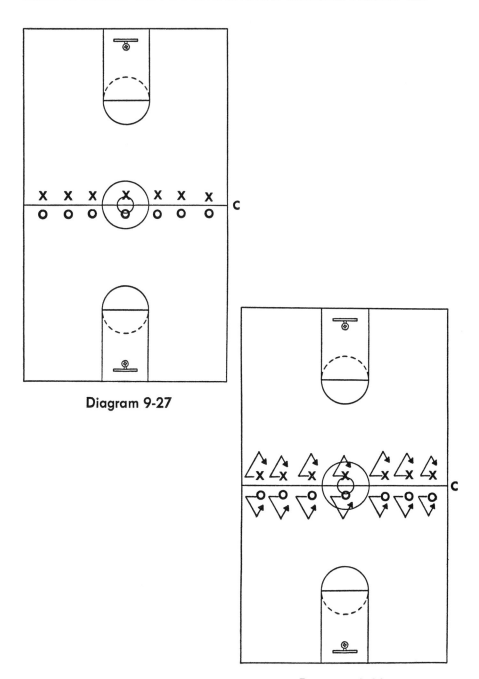

Diagram 9-27

Diagram 9-28

hand motion of the actor line to be emulated by the reactor line (Diagram 9-28).

This drill is also an excellent drill for agility and coordination. In executing the 1-3-1 zone defenses, it is of the utmost importance that each individual player possesses quick reactions and excellent footwork.

The "Cage" Drill

We utilize the "cage" drill to teach the area responsibilities and defensive slides of the defensive point man 1. 1, the defensive point man, is positioned in the defensive floor area that we refer to as his "cage" (Diagram 9-29).

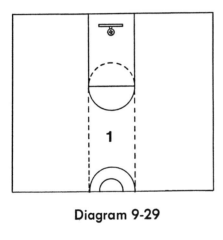

Diagram 9-29

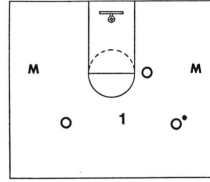

Diagram 9-30

The drill begins with two offensive players positioned with the ball out front. Offensive guards will be used to attack the point man in this drill. An offensive post man will be positioned at a high side post position with freedom of movement to each side of the lane. Also, managers will be positioned at each wing position (Diagram 9-30).

The defensive point man 1, varying his defensive floor position, must prevent a direct guard-to-guard pass. The only passes the offensive players are allowed to make are bounce passes and lob passes. The offensive guards advance the ball from mid-court and the point man attacks them aggressively positioning himself between them, isolating the ball on one side of the floor. The offensive guards must execute one guard-to-guard pass after meeting resistance from 1. After the pass, they can feed a manager positioned at a wing position who looks to feed the offensive player at the high post (Diagram 9-31).

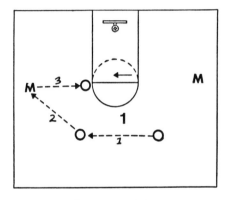

Diagram 9-31

The defensive point man 1, on the flight of the ball to the wing position, must quickly release and prevent the pass from the wing to the high post (Diagram 9-32).

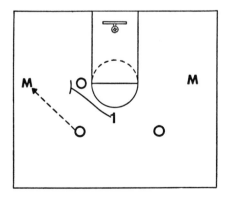

Diagram 9-32

After the guard-to-wing pass is executed, the defensive point man 1 protects the high post area. The ball at the wing position is passed back to the guard who attempts to reverse the ball to the opposite guard. 1, who is fronting the side high post position, on the flight of the ball from the wing out to the guard, must quickly move into a defensive floor position and again prevent the direct guard-to-guard pass (Diagram 9-33).

In the event that the direct pass is made from guard to guard and the offense is successful in getting the ball into the high post man, then we start the drill over again.

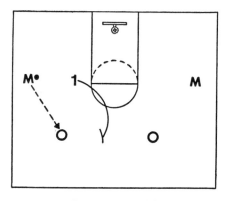

Diagram 9-33

Note: This drill can also be run on both ends of the floor and the defensive point slides and responsibilities can be taught at two different stations.

Competition is added to this drill by allowing each defensive point man to defend five times against the offense. For each direct guard-to-guard pass and for each successful pass from the wing to the high post, the point man must run one sprinter or "killer" drill. While they are running, the next defensive point man steps in and the drill continues.

Perimeter Defensive Drill

This is a defensive drill that is excellent for developing defensive coordination between the defensive point man and the defensive wing men. The initial alignment of the drill is set up with the defensive point man 1 and the defensive wing men 3 and 4 in their defensive positions. Two offensive players (guards) with the ball are positioned outside. They should be active and are allowed to penetrate if the opportunity presents itself. Two additional offensive players are positioned on each side of the baseline area. They are allowed only to receive a pass and return it. *They are not* active (Diagram 9-34).

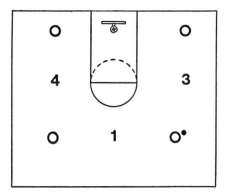

Diagram 9-34

The defensive point man 1 should vary his initial defensive position. He should eliminate the direct or quick guard-to-guard pass. The wing man on the ball side of the floor comes up and applies pressure to the ball whenever the offensive player with the ball comes into his area. The defensive point man helps 3 if the offensive player attempts to penetrate. 1 aligns himself with the line of the ball to prevent the direct guard-to-guard pass (Diagram 9-35).

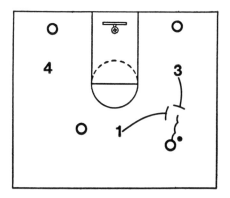

Diagram 9-35

If the offensive guard passes to the opposite guard, 4, the defensive wing man off the ball comes up to apply pressure while 1, the defensive point man aligns himself in the passing lane (Diagram 9-36).

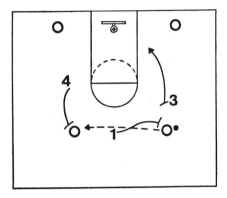

Diagram 9-36

In the event the offensive guard with the ball elects to pass the ball to the baseline, the defensive wing man 3 or 4, depending on which side of the floor the ball is, can sag to protect the high lane area and 1 will play the passing lane between the guards. The defensive wing men can elect to overplay the passing lanes from the base line back out front and allow 1 to sag and protect the high lane area (Diagram 9-37).

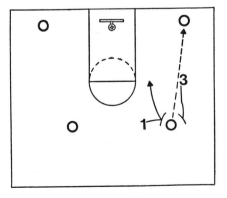

Diagram 9-37

Note: The coach should stop the drill at any time and correct the body angles and defensive responsibilities of the defensive point man and wing man. After the drill has progressed and the defensive slides and responsibilities are learned, a stationary offensive high post man can be added to the drill.

The Pivot Penetration Reaction Drill

This is a drill we utilize to develop the defensive reaction of our pivot man 5. Our pivot man is the "hub" of our 1-3-1 zone defense and one of his prime responsibilities is to help stop any penetration by the offensive team. In order to accomplish this, we must drill our pivot man in stopping penetration and simulate the offensive situations he must defend against.

The drill begins with the pivot man 5 setting up his regular floor position in the 1-3-1 zone defense. Two offensive players are positioned out front with the basketball and an offensive player is positioned on each block (Diagram 9-38).

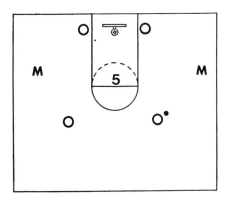

Diagram 9-38

Note: Two managers also position themselves in this drill on each side of the floor.

The drill begins with the two offensive players out front passing the basketball back and forth, and then one of them attempts to penetrate with the ball. The defensive pivot man who has moved from side to side while the offensive players were passing the ball out front, upon seeing the offensive man attempt to dribble-penetrate, comes up quick with his hands up and with a wide defensive base (Diagram 9-39).

Note: We instruct 5, the pivot man, to react quickly and come up and put his "numbers" (chest) on the ball.

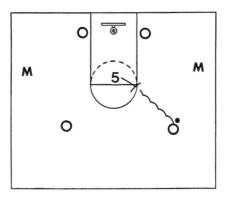

Diagram 9-39

The offensive player with the ball who has attempted penetration, upon being stopped by the pivot man, quickly passes the ball to one of the managers on his side of the floor. The manager catches the ball and attempts to pass it to the offensive player positioned on the block. The defensive pivot man 5, upon stopping offensive penetration, releases upon the flight of the ball from the offensive player to the manager and sprints to deflect or intercept the pass from the manager to the offensive man positioned on the block (Diagram 9-40).

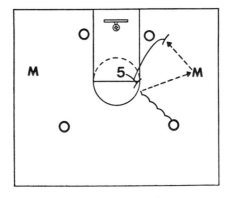

Diagram 9-40

This drill simulates the most difficult defensive responsibility of the pivot man 5 in the 1-3-1 zone defense. He must be drilled to react quickly to this offensive situation as it is extremely difficult to defend against.

Note: This drill can be set up on both ends of the floor and run at two different stations.

"Body Angle" Drill

This is an excellent defensive drill that can be utilized by teams employing any type of pressure zone defense. The drill emphasizes and teaches defensive wing players to maintain good defensive body angles between the ball and the baseline.

As we stated earlier, the body angles of the defensive players are of extreme importance to the success of the pressure-type zone defenses.

The drill is composed of two defensive wing men, two offensive guards out front with the ball and two offensive players along the baseline (Diagram 9-41).

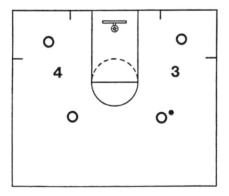

Diagram 9-41

Note: The offensive players on the baseline are allowed to move only inside the area indicated by the hash marks in the diagram.

The drill begins with one of the offensive guards with the ball out front moving and attempting to execute a direct pass to the offensive players on his side of the floor. The defensive wing man 3 becomes very active with hands up and feet moving while applying good pressure to the ball. He should maintain a good body angle to prevent the direct pass to the baseline. The defensive wing man must be alert to the position of the ball and also the movement and position of the offensive player on the baseline in order to block the passing lane to the baseline (Diagram 9-42).

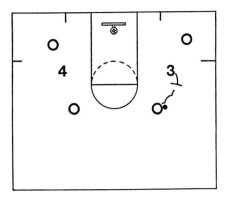

Diagram 9-42

Note: The only passes the defensive wing men should permit the offense to make are bounce passes or lob passes. These are the slowest passes in basketball and permit the offense time to recover.

The offensive guards out front can reverse the ball at any time and attack from the opposite side of the floor; the defensive wing men must be alert for this game-type action.

In the event that the ball is passed to the baseline, the defensive wing man turns and positions his body in the passing lane from the baseline to the offensive guard out front. He again must be alert to the position of the ball and the floor position of the guard out front.

The "I" Drill

The "I" drill is one we utilize to strengthen the middle of the 1-3-1 zone defenses. It is excellent for developing the defensive reactions, floor awareness and coordinated movements of the point man, center or middle man and the baseline man in the 1-3-1 zone defenses. The old baseball axiom, "you must be strong up the middle defensively" very definitely applies to the 1-3-1 zone defenses in basketball.

The "I" drill is set up with the defensive point man 1, the defensive center or middle man 5 and the baseline man 2 aligned in their defensive positions. Their initial defensive alignment forms an "I," thus our naming of the drill (Diagram 9-43).

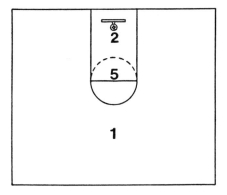

Diagram 9-43

Five players are involved in this drill, two offensive guards out front with the ball, two offensive players on the baseline and an offensive player at the high post opposite the ball (Diagram 9-44).

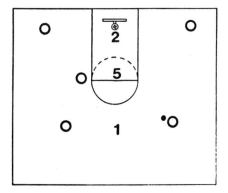

Diagram 9-44

The drill begins with the ball passed from an offensive guard to the baseline. The defensive baseline man 2 releases on the flight of the ball to the baseline and moves out to defend the corner area. The center or middle man also on the flight of the ball quickly slides and fronts or protects the block area underneath the basket. The defensive point man 1, with the ball on the baseline, slides down and defends the high post area (Diagram 9-45).

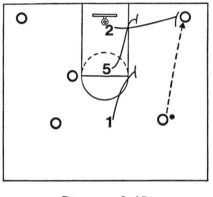

Diagram 9-45

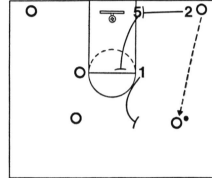

Diagram 9-46

Note: The offensive players opposite the ball can move or flash to the ball side of the floor at any time during the drill. For example, the opposite offensive baseline player can flash underneath the basket to the block area (5 must be alert for this) and the offensive high post man opposite the ball can flash to the ball at any time (1 must be alert for this).

Whenever the ball is passed outside from the baseline, the defensive point man 1, who is sagging to defend the high post area, must quickly move out and prevent a direct guard-to-guard pass. 5, who is defending the block area, quickly moves back up to his initial defensive position. 2, who is defending the corner area, on the flight of the ball outside from the baseline, quickly moves back to his initial baseline position with his inside foot in the lane area defending the block area (Diagram 9-46).

The "Diamond" Trapping Drill

This is a drill we employ to develop the successful execution of double-teaming or trapping the offensive player with the basketball. Since the 1-3-1 trapping defense is an intregral part of our defensive arsenal, it is imperative that the defensive players are fundamentally sound in executing defensive double-teams and traps.

The "Diamond" Trapping Drill is set up with four defensive players, the defensive point man, two defensive wing men and the defensive baseline man (1, 3, 4, and 2). The initial defensive alignment of the players forming a diamond type alignment gives the drill its name (Diagram 9-47).

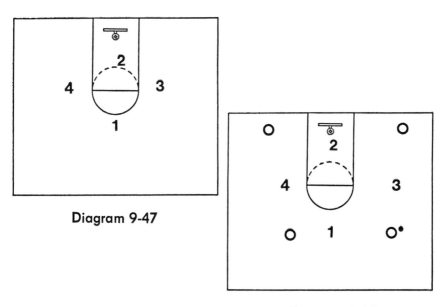

Diagram 9-47

Diagram 9-48

Note: The post man 5 is not utilized in this drill, in order to permit offensive penetration with the ball by the offensive players and force the four defensive players to react quickly and execute fundamentally sound double-teams and traps on the basketball.

Four offensive players are also involved in the drill, two offensive guards out front and two forwards on the deep wings and baseline (Diagram 9-48).

On the coach's whistle, the drill begins with the ball outside at a guard position. The defensive point man 1 prevents the direct guard-to-guard pass and plays the ball square. The defensive forward 3 comes up quickly maintaining a good body angle and applies a double-team with 1 (Diagram 9-49).

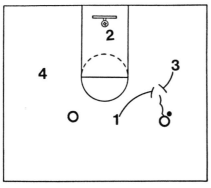

Diagram 9-49

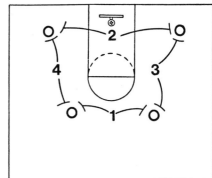

Diagram 9-50

The four offensive players attempt to penetrate with the ball and prevent the double-teams or traps. They also attempt to penetrate and execute a quick direct or line-drive type pass to a teammate.

The defensive players must execute four double-teams or traps out front and on the baseline while allowing the offensive players to execute only bounce passes or lob passes to teammates. Diagram 9-50 illustrates the double-teams or traps executed on both sides of the floor.

In the event that the defense is successful in their defensive execution, they are awarded one point on a competitive basis. The initial offensive players have five possessions and then the defense switches to offense and the offense switches to defense. The competition continues and the team compiling the highest defensive proficiency wins, with sprints or "killer" drills for the losing team.

Index